All Abou Poetry !

CU00905672

Northern England

Edited by
Helen Davies

This book belongs to

First published in Great Britain in 2010 by

 Young**Writers**

Remus House
Coltsfoot Drive
Peterborough
PE2 9JX
Telephone: 01733 890066
Website: www.youngwriters.co.uk

Foreword

At Young Writers our defining aim is to promote an enjoyment of reading and writing amongst children and young adults. By giving aspiring poets the opportunity to see their work in print, their love of the written word as well as confidence in their own abilities has the chance to blossom.

Our latest competition *Poetry Express* was designed to introduce primary school children to the wonders of creative expression. They were given free reign to write on any theme and in any style, thus encouraging them to use and explore a variety of different poetic forms.

We are proud to present the resulting collection of regional anthologies which are an excellent showcase of young writing talent. With such a diverse range of entries received, the selection process was difficult yet very rewarding.

From comical rhymes to poignant verses, there is plenty to entertain and inspire within these pages. We hope you agree that this collection bursting with imagination is one to treasure.

Contents

**St Mary's RC Primary School,
Newcastle upon Tyne**

**St Paul's RC Primary School,
Billingham**

The Poems

Walking On The Edge

Walking near the sea
Splashing in the waves
Every step I take towards the cliffs
Each footprint that it saves.

Which way do I go?
What path should I choose?
It only takes one mistake
And that's everything I lose.

Should I run back
Or run up the hill?
For the rest of my life
I'll just be standing still.

As I walk, I leave a trail
The sand tickles my toes
And the smell of sea salt
Also tickles my nose.

Soon the waves close in
The time left is short
So I go home to rest
My feet got to port.

Sian Huckle (11)
Bader Primary School, Thornaby

Footprints · Where Did They Go?

The sunlight beams down on the golden sand,
Where my footprints leave a trail.
They start to go to the left, then turn right.
They start to go forward,
Suddenly they chance and then turn back.
Then the wind blows, blowing them away.
Is the wind blowing my life away?
I don't know where to go!
Backwards?
Forwards?
Left
Or right?
Do I go anywhere
Or should I just wait?
Will someone save me or will I be alone?
I want to find my way home but . . .
I can't find my way there
Because my footprints are gone!

Rees Miller (10)
Bader Primary School, Thornaby

Predatory Dragon

Head charging
Eyes glowing
Teeth grinding
Mouth slavering
Breath firing
Ears twitching
Claws grating
Tail flicking.

Chloe Goult (9)
Bader Primary School, Thornaby

Footprints

I think of my life as a disgrace
And all the terrible things I have done
Most of my footprints disappear
Is it too late? What should I do?
The sun is nearly down
Does this mean the end?
Must I turn back or should I just quit?
I don't know.
The sun has now vanished
Now I just wait
Goodbye.

Jake Thompson (10)
Bader Primary School, Thornaby

Dragon Movements

Mouth opening
Eyes trespassing
Tail soaring
Head swirling
Spikes spearing
Ears twitching
Breath breezing
And claws gripping.

Aden Smiles (8)
Bader Primary School, Thornaby

Leave Me Alone

I am the biggest,
The mighty,
The king.

Yet a cold heart
Of ice
I want to be left alone
I'm cold, angry and spiteful.

Higher than all,
Top mountain,
I reach above the clouds,
I'm huge,
Caped with crystals
That come from above.

Those ants come,
Stabbing me,
With their metal equipment,
I howl in pain
And crumble!

But I will protest,
I cough,
My icy breath,
Down!
They are suffocated
From the cold.
The storm clouds,
Help me!

They disperse them back,
Anything . . .
Anything
That falls on me
Will get swallowed
Whole!

I will be left
Alone.

Naeema Chowdhury (10)
Benton Park Primary School, Newcastle

The Lonely Mountain

I am immeasurable
Few people conquer me
I am strong
Legs covered in dark forest.

I am lonely
My eyes see everything
I feel sad
I want friends
I cry out . . .
No one listens
They run away.

Small children playing
Tickling my toes
My body getting older
Wrinkles appearing *rapidly*
My fingers dancing impatiently.

I hear the flying chair
Bringing chattering, excited voices
I hear the whistling wind
As it says, 'Hello!'

Jamie Danjoux (11)
Benton Park Primary School, Newcastle

Mountain Loneliness

I hear the wind
Whispering, 'Hello.'
Birds singing
People look at me in disgust
I feel like crying

I am the strongest
Most confident peak
You'll ever meet
But inside
I'm very soft, soft as a new teddy

I am stuck here
Alone
No one cares about me
No one will
I'm alone

My body has holes, cracks
When people are unaware
My mouth opens
Dinner down in one
People think of me as dangerous
However, people still attempt
The climb
Not many have succeeded
Not many!

I'm never going to be moved
I need something
Other than my reflection
I need someone
Something
I'm lonely.

Sophie Delaney (10)
Benton Park Primary School, Newcastle

The Undiscovered Range

I love my life
It's great being undiscovered
Friends in the sky cry white tears above you
You don't worry about swallowing people
People falling off your head
Or getting lost in your feet
You have many pets
You have a massive garden
Everyone cares for you

I am happy with many friends
I'm sometimes miserable
People want to climb other mountains
It's not fair!
I'm very *important*
I'm a refuge
I'm an animal refuge
I'm proud to be me

I hear everything in the outside world
I've been told that:
Last year, a volcano erupted
Two days ago, K2 was conquered
And in this range a new mountain was formed
I have the best hearing

Many animals suffer
The panda is starving
Snow leopards have trouble catching prey
Birds have trouble migrating
I try my best to help
I still love my life.

Tate Mukanganiki (10)
Benton Park Primary School, Newcastle

Mountain Feelings

I feel lonely
Nobody has come up
And said, 'Hello!'
I just want a friend
I am *not* deadly.
People just come up halfway
And go back down
I don't mean to kill people,
They just slip into my mouth.
I feel unloved
Now I'm *angry* and *furious.*

I hear screams
From boys and girls
Screaming and shouting at me
I hear snow leopards and bears
Roaring and
Clawing me!
Clawing me whilst ripping me apart
I hear people whispering things about me
Like, 'Ugly, good for nothing'
And other *horrible* things.
I feel *miserable.*

All I see is
Trees and flowers talking about me
But then I see my reflection. On the lake.
I'm all *broken!*
I look ugly and *beastly!*
I have become a *monster!*

Adeeb Rahman (10)
Benton Park Primary School, Newcastle

My Mountain Life!

I'm tall, but small
Smaller than the rest
I'm not *tough*
I'm *skinny*
But for some I'm a test
Other mountains think they can dominate me
But I soon push them off

Trees surround me
In their thousands
Dancing side to side
Making me jealous of their friendship

Day by day
People stab me
Trying to reach my top
I hear them grunting
As they struggle
To reach my summit top

The others make me feel
I don't exist
They make my life
Miserable

I wish one day
I'm part of a group of friends
Who care for each other
And treat each other
Exactly the same.

Gaurav Chaddah (11)
Benton Park Primary School, Newcastle

Left In Peace

I just want to be left in peace
Because
Family
Dead
Crushed
With the mountaineers.
Their metal spikes dug into our skulls
But we couldn't fight back
You were too many.

I don't want to be climbed upon
I want peace
Please
Please leave me in peace
I don't want to do something I'll regret.

The mountaineers don't care about us
They think we haven't got a heart
Well, they're wrong
They're all wrong
Some of us don't mean to swallow them whole
And blow them off us
It's just we're trying to protect ourselves
But if you don't want to be killed
Leave
Us
In
Peace!

Lindsay Saint (11)
Benton Park Primary School, Newcastle

I'm Just A Lonely Mountain!

I stand over Legoland
Watching mountains
I am peaceful
But . . .
When people step on my peak
Tickle my hair cheek
I laugh as they fall down

I look like a beast
But I'm isolated
I don't chatter with other mountains
I sit snoozing
The wind awakes me
He starts to whisper
I can't understand
What he's saying!

I get comfort
By tiny people shouting and having adventures
I'm heartbroken
When I hear,
'Bye for now.' That's my fear!

I don't mind people using me however
They poke me and stab me
My skin will crack
I start to cry
My tears wash the skiers down.

Kristen Lea Watson (10)
Benton Park Primary School, Newcastle

Me: The Mountain

I am colourful like a rainbow,
Bright and beautiful.
I am friendly,
People *don't* believe me!
I am perceived as being dangerous
Fierce and mighty!
It was an accident
I didn't *mean* to gobble those people,
They just fell into my mouth!

As the seasons change
So do my sights
I squint to see through the snow
The rivers always freeze
It's the opposite in summer
The streams flow again
Then I see my reflection
With water I feed to the river every day.

When I look down to see the wind chattering
Chattering to the trees,
I feel left by myself,
Alone,
No friends,
Everyone leaves me out.
They think I have no feelings,
They mistake me.

Lauren Boyle (10)
Benton Park Primary School, Newcastle

I'm A Lonely Mountain

I cry every day
I'm isolated from my kind
People think of me as nothing
Disregard me as important

Sophisticated and proud I seem
But I'm lonely inside
When the metal tools pierce my flesh
I feel abused

My heart becomes more disheartened
Each day
As my body crumbles
Away

Eagles circle my head
Mocking my loneliness
The animals beneath socialise to each other
I long for the day
I can meet people like me

I look down at my reflection
Solemnly
I ponder deeply to myself
Will I forever be
Lonely?

Taku Mandishonha (11)
Benton Park Primary School, Newcastle

I Stand Alone

I am fierce
Fierce I am
Guarded
Guarded by Hell
I was not born this way
But made this way
Made by you.

I was once happy
White clouds
Tourists
All you can imagine
Then I was surrounded
Surrounded by stormy clouds
Thunder
And lightning.

Now you're gone
All I wish for
Is a friend
A friend that doesn't judge
I am a mountain
A mountain like the others
Yet different.

Lauren Olivia Walker (10)
Benton Park Primary School, Newcastle

Standing Alone!

I am alone
All on my own
Storm clouds are my bodyguards
They let no trespassers up to me
Just one tiny step
And
Thunder
Lightning
Scares them away

I am alone
All on my own
How I wish I had a friend
I ask my bodyguards
Why can't they stay?
They answer back
They will crush you
With their fierce climbing ways
Yet, still I don't understand
All I want is some company.

Verity Alderman (10)
Benton Park Primary School, Newcastle

I Am A Mountain

I am a mountain,
I am.
Black clouds
Surround me
Suffocate me
But I will fight strong.

Hard as nails,
Waiting.
Waiting for travellers to try and conquer me
But I will swallow them whole,
Digesting them to my bottomless pit.

I am a mountain,
I am.
Some day for this I rise
Rise up bigger and stronger than ever before,.
Standing,
Always standing,
Invincible.

Thomas Potts (10)
Benton Park Primary School, Newcastle

Surrounded!

I am the fierce king
Crowned in white
A single mountain
Single
But surrounded
By you
Mountaineers
You're at risk
My stomach rumbles
The trap is set
I'll swallow you whole
You have been warned
You make me angry
It's not my fault
I don't deserve this
Leave me alone
Or feel my wrath . . .

Leah Gardiner (11)
Benton Park Primary School, Newcastle

What A Mountain Feels!

I stand *alone*
Feeling cut off from the rest of the *world*
My feet moulded to the ground
I wish I could walk around
To see the rest of my species

Sometimes mountaineers climb me
They tickle my nose
I can't help but . . . *sneeze!*

I look at my reflection in the sparkling pond
Below I see a lonely mountain
That needs taking care of
People never ask me how *I* feel
As they're sliding down my rocky skin
I wear a white snow hat
Stretching across my rough body.

Katrina Affleck (10)
Benton Park Primary School, Newcastle

My New Life As A Mountain

Many have fallen into my hands
Few have been accepted
Powerful, mighty,
Like a bird patiently watching its prey

I stand alone
Isolated
Stronger than ever
Pickaxes slashing through my body
Tearing at my soul

Watching my reflection in the lake
Oh, how the years have changed me
Skin falling apart
Old and withered
Crumbling.

Syed Naeeb Zahed (9)
Benton Park Primary School, Newcastle

Global Warming

G reat is our Earth
L onely it's becoming
O blivious with the damage we are doing
B elieve me, we can help
A fter all, we have to save our Earth
L ive in it with love and care

W e can help save it
A ll of us together
R epair this damage we have done
M other Nature can't do it all
I t needs our help
N ever give up
G reat is our Earth.

Aysha Mughal (8)
Chorlton Park Primary School, Manchester

Train

I am going on a train tonight
And I am very excited
But it's still very light
On the train.

I am going on a train,
How many stations will we stop at?
I will have lots of fun,
Oh look, there is a lady with a big hat.
I will have the best time ever.
Now we arrive, I wonder who I will see?
I think the train was great fun
Who will pick me up, Trevor or Lee?
I wonder what other transport there would be?
Aeroplane,
Helicopter or car?
But I still like the train.
As we have had a safe journey on the train,
Choo, choo, choo, choo.
Next time it might be a plane,
My journey.

Krystal Swali (8)
Chorlton Park Primary School, Manchester

Superhero

Once I was a superhero
Once I could fly into the sky
Once I was a superhero
Once I could save lives and somebody's wife
Once I was a superhero
Once I could catch bad guys and spare their lives.

Sankalp Soni (9)
Chorlton Park Primary School, Manchester

Untitled

The sky is white
I wonder why?
The ground is white
I wonder why?
Look all around you, it has come again
And you wonder why?

White is purity
And pure you are
When it is cold
There is no one about
Let the king and queen
Practise their descent upon
The Earth
Yes, when there is no one about.

Kaydiah Henry (9)
Chorlton Park Primary School, Manchester

My Chickens

Peck, peck, peck, pecking on the door,
Scratch, scratch, scratch, scratching on the floor.
I love my chickens
They make me smile.

Yum, yum, yum, eggs for tea
The biggest yolk you'll ever see.
I love my chickens
With their red combs on top.

The feathers on their bottom go *wiggle, wiggle, wiggle,*
And me and my sisters go, *giggle, giggle, giggle.*
I love my chickens
And they love me.

Josh Fox (9)
Chorlton Park Primary School, Manchester

A Friend And A Gem

I have this friend Ruby, who is such a gem
So here are some things that are the same about them

A gem is so beautiful and calm
But my friend Ruby, she's always jumping around

They're so nice and glittery
As well as this they just like to be fluttery

My best friend Ruby, she is so rare
Just like the gem that sparkles everywhere

Now just to finish off my lovely poem
I'd like to say how much I want to be with them.

Atalanta Sawdon Harkavy (9)
Chorlton Park Primary School, Manchester

Racing Cars

Zooming cars around the track,
People cheer when they come near,
When they crash, that's that,
They can't come back on the racing track!

Powerful upgrades boost their speed,
And that's what they'll need to stay in the lead!
Zooming cars around the track
The king of the cars always comes back!

Samori Weekes (8)
Chorlton Park Primary School, Manchester

Tudors · Cinquain

Tudors
Elizabeth
Edward and Mary too
And don't forget Henry's head was
Chopped off.

Ayan Bukhari (9)
Chorlton Park Primary School, Manchester

Pizzas · Cinquain

Pizzas
Are nice to eat
Toppings: Ham, pineapple
Put in the oven then eat it
Pizzas.

Charlotte Tonner (9)
Chorlton Park Primary School, Manchester

School · Cinquain

Keyboard
It's fun and new
Reading, laughing, writing
You have 6 new messages on
Email.

Assl Sarmad Al-Dulaimi (9)
Chorlton Park Primary School, Manchester

Bats · Haiku

Here I am flying,
My colour is night, pitch-black,
People say I'm blind.

India Sangar (8)
Chorlton Park Primary School, Manchester

Monsters · Haiku

Monsters: very bad
Monsters thumping, stamping now
Monsters, monsters, *'Roar!'*

Hooriya Mahmood (8)
Chorlton Park Primary School, Manchester

Little Ladybird

Little ladybird
Crawling along my fingers
Red and black
With a dotty back
Sweet, shiny, red ladybird
Are a good gardener's friend
When you are with me
The fun never ends
They munch and crunch little nasty beasts
While soaking up the sun
Scurrying around
They don't make a sound
When they are done
And have finished their fun
They fly away in the breeze
Come back ladybird, please.

Jasmine Tew (9)
Hungerford Primary School, Crewe

Shopping

S lowly looking round the toys
H olding things you're not allowed to have
O pening things when you aren't supposed to
P ennies all over the place
P opping in and out of shops
I can't decide what to buy
N otes hanging out of your purse
G etting ready to spend, spend, spend.

Connie Porter (8)
Hungerford Primary School, Crewe

Space

Roving Rover
Spinning sun
Moving moon
Flaming rocks
Sand sun
Cosmic comets
Banning room
Sparkling sapphire
Fast blast
Whooshing wind
Zooming space belt
Bright burning.

Sophie Stiff (10)
Lingdale Primary School, Lingdale

Space

Brown Jupiter
Hot sun
Yellow sun
Silver stars
Orange Saturn
Blue Uranus
Black hole
Dazzling stars
Beautiful stars
Small Pluto
Blue and green Earth
Bright sun.

Leona Hindson (8)
Lingdale Primary School, Lingdale

Space

Dazzling stars
Rocking planets
Hot planets
Cold planets
Awesome zero gravity
Rocky Mars
Rocky Pluto
Red Mars
Awesome spacemen
Brave spacemen
Neil Armstrong
Buzz Aldrin.

Ben Hadley (9)
Lingdale Primary School, Lingdale

Space

Red Mars
Pretty stars
Hot sun
Burning fun
Black hole
White pole
Lovely Milky Way
Go away
Big comets
Bigger rockets
Orange Saturn
Nice pattern.

Megan Greensmith (9)
Lingdale Primary School, Lingdale

Stars

Really warm
Scalds all
Big bang
Deafening sound
Red ruby
Astonishing light
Very old
Big holes
Hydraulic gas
Great mass
Sparkling bright
Huge light.

Billy Scott (10)
Lingdale Primary School, Lingdale

Space

Cold Pluto
Weird looking
Dazzling
Hot Mercury
Lifelike Earth
Gassy Venus
Massive Jupiter
Topsy-turvy Uranus
Mysterious Neptune
Spooky moon
Awesome spacemen
Hot asteroids.

Aidan Bennison (10)
Lingdale Primary School, Lingdale

Space

Red Mars
Dazzling stars
Milky Milky Way
Go away
Hot sun
Funny fun
Black hole
White pole
Rocky rockets
Silly comets
Brown Saturn
Pretty pattern.

Holly Hurst (9)
Lingdale Primary School, Lingdale

Space

Bright stars
Brown comets
Hot sun
Coloured planets
Large planets
Tiny planets
Black gap
Rocky rocket
Stone planets
Dazzling Milky Way
Happy spaceman.

Charlie Templeman (9)
Lingdale Primary School, Lingdale

Stars

Gleaming bright
Giant light
Glowing high
Sparkling sky
Moon, white
Only night
Millions glowing
Shining jewel
Little gems
Flashing diamond.

Owen Treloar (9)
Lingdale Primary School, Lingdale

Space

Human suffocater
Rocky planets
Blasting asteroids
Dazzling stars
Flaming sun
Swirly Milky Way
Massive Mercury
Gloomy galaxy
Zooming comet
Sizzling sun.

Shannon Rogerson (9)
Lingdale Primary School, Lingdale

Stars

Fast blast
Sparkling stars
Far away
Dark sky
Shining light
Spooky sky
Freezing planet
Hot planet
Weird planet
Scary planet.

Kieran Ryan (10)
Lingdale Primary School, Lingdale

Planets

Big fuzz
Small clang
Old bang
Young pile
Heavy, big
Cold, light
Large gases
Hard rock
Clingy cling
Fizzy, hot.

Casey Stonehouse (9)
Lingdale Primary School, Lingdale

Space

Fast blast
Rocket crashed
Burning sun
Having fun
Shooting stars
Red Mars
Black hole
Freezing cold
Flashing lights
Every night.

Adele Scott (9)
Lingdale Primary School, Lingdale

Space

Super Saturn
Cold planets
Super gravity
Dazzling stars
Rocky moon
Rocking rockets
Glistening space belt
Shimmering sun
Fire burning
Vicious Venus.

Harley Jackson (9)
Lingdale Primary School, Lingdale

The Moon

Bumpy golf ball
Silky snowball
Soft hammock
Silky sand.

Shining star
Hard marble
It is a ball
Sparkling icicle
Stone-cold rock.

Kai Colman (8)
Lingdale Primary School, Lingdale

Space

Death stars
Gas attack
Rocky rockets
Rocky planets
The big black hole
Cosmic comets
The bite white hole
Saturday Saturn
Milky, Milky Way.

Jay Clayton (9)
Lingdale Primary School, Lingdale

The Moon

Silky snowball
White ghost
Hard, crystal ball
White frost.

Gleaming coin
Holey cheese
Dusty ball
Stinky cheese.

Jade Stiff (7)
Lingdale Primary School, Lingdale

The Moon

Silky snowball
Shimmering spheres
Hard, crystal ball
Sparkling circle.

Bumpy golf ball
Silky diamond
Hard stone
Bouncy hammock.

Hollie Serginson (8)
Lingdale Primary School, Lingdale

The Moon

Silky snowball
Smooth marble
Round orange
Bumpy golf ball.

Bouncy trampoline
Dark night
Rough brick
Stone-cold rock.

Callum Moorhouse (8)
Lingdale Primary School, Lingdale

The Moon

Soft hammock
Shining icicle
Sparkling diamond
White ghost
Damp rock
Cheesy.

Shay Harris (8)
Lingdale Primary School, Lingdale

The Moon

Smooth marble
Silky snowball
Gleaming coin
Glistening snowflake.

Bumpy golf ball
Stone-cold rock
Rough brick
Hard diamond.

Kieran Wren (8)
Lingdale Primary School, Lingdale

The Moon

Glistening snowball
Soft hammock
Shiny light
White marble.

White frost
Silky snowball
Sparkling snow
Gleaming coin.

Abbie Bennison (9)
Lingdale Primary School, Lingdale

The Moon

Bumpy golf ball
Silky snowball
Stone-cold rock
Bright marble.

Hard crystal ball
Shining light bulb
Glistening sphere
Enormous cheese.

Jake Gilpin (8)
Lingdale Primary School, Lingdale

The Moon

White golf ball
Stone-cold rock
Soft hammock
White marble
Glistening snowball
Shining coin
Hard crystal ball
Silky, soft blanket.

Jodie McSorley (7)
Lingdale Primary School, Lingdale

Untitled

A frog can jump onto a lily pad
A sheep can leap onto the grass
A horse can run and it can trot
A rabbit can pounce on its prey
An ant can crawl in the hall.

Lucy Smith, Oliver Stroh, Leo (5), Ned & William (6)
Long Preston Primary School, Skipton

Ronnie Rabbit

On Monday, Ronnie ran across the roof
And the roof is waterproof
On Tuesday, Ronnie was on a sleigh
Singing a song, hip hip hooray
On Wednesday, Ronnie went to a farm
He was milking a cow - *wow!*
On Thursday, Ronnie went for a drive in his shiny red car
His tyre was flat and he didn't get far
On Friday, Ronnie rode a sheep
And he fell in a heap.

**Lewis Hooley (7) William Daley, Harris Dinsdale,
Harry Mathew & Laura Birrell (6)**
Long Preston Primary School, Skipton

Twirly Whirly

Twirly Whirly lives in a ship
And he has a pink lip
The lip bursts and has a snap
The cat is surprised and slips off his lap
He is slimy and shimmery
And shouts, 'I'm scary!'
Watch out for Twirly Whirly
He is a bit of a girly!

Simran Thomas (6)
Long Preston Primary School, Skipton

The Go Pop Go

There is a Go Pop Go
He lives on Mars
He'll eat anything that comes in a bar
Children, cats and mice
As long as it tastes nice!
He has a slimy green face
And vanishes without a trace
Watch out for the Go Pop Go!

Isobel Birrell (7)
Long Preston Primary School, Skipton

Guinea Pigs

My guinea pigs are great pets
They hardly have to go to the vets
Guinea pigs have lots of fur
And when they're happy they love to purr.

Becky Smith (6)
Long Preston Primary School, Skipton

Mouse

Mice eat cheese
And they never say please
Mice like to squeak
From their hut they peek.

Luke Beresford (6)
Long Preston Primary School, Skipton

Dog

Dogs love walks
And bark when they talk
Dogs have a wet nose
And they doze.

Matthew Mandziuk (5)
Long Preston Primary School, Skipton

Cow

Cows go moo
What do they do?
Cows make cheese
And they have knobbly knees.

George Fitton (7)
Long Preston Primary School, Skipton

Cats
(Dedicated to my grandma, Yvonne Betsy McCartney)

Knee-jumper
Claw-scratcher
Paw-licker
Vicious-snarler
Horrible-hisser
Hair-leaver
Toy-player
Little-lover.

Olivia Edwards (10)
Newcastle Church High School, Newcastle upon Tyne

My Baby

Bed-wetter
Midnight-screamer
Innocent-smiler
TV-starer
Nose-biter
Dreaming-dribbler
Head-butter
Thrower-upper
What am I?

Tari Angelica Mahofa (11)
Newcastle Church High School, Newcastle upon Tyne

My Brother

Teddy-killer
Malteser-stealer
Chocolate-scoffer
Mischief-maker
Two-year-old-actor
Bedtime-scarer
TV-starer
Xbox-player.

Jessica Rankin (11)
Newcastle Church High School, Newcastle upon Tyne

A Puppy

Tail-wagger
Bone-muncher
Walk-wisher
Toy-ripper
Treats-lover
Dangerous-snapper
Occasional-whiffer
Little-runner.

Charlotte Cowell (10)
Newcastle Church High School, Newcastle upon Tyne

Coal

Bright-shiner
Yellow-dimmer
Orange-glower
Red-burner
Grey-ender
Burn-creator
Ember-jumper
Black-suiter.

Skye Costelloe (11)
Newcastle Church High School, Newcastle upon Tyne

Or Ponies?

... licker
Salt licker
Leg leaper
Polo eater
Knee wobbler
Hay demolisher
Giant jumper
Bit muncher.

Anna Munro (10)
Newcastle Church High School, Newcastle upon Tyne

The Horse

Ear-twitcher
Fast-trotter
Tail-swisher
Proud-prancer
Hay-champer
Lively-leaper
Shoulder-stretcher
Mint-muncher.

Amy Cook (10)
Newcastle Church High School, Newcastle upon Tyne

Battlefield

Lots of machinery all around
Bombs dropping on the ground
Gunfire never-ending
Steel girders twisting and bending
Looks like this war will never end.

Matthew Clark (9)
North & South Cowton Community Primary School, Northallerton

My Dreams

When I fall asleep at night
I think of anything
Playing sports, having drinks, eating food
And . . . then come the nightmares.
Getting struck by lightning
Dying monsters, aliens, zombies, skeletons
Poisonous snakes, then when the going gets scary
You wake up and go into your mum and dad's room
And . . . they tell you to go back to bed.
You go back to sleep and think of playing football
For a professional football team
In the World Cup final against Germany
And . . . you get the winning goal
Playing for the England cricket team
You're bowling on the last ball
You need a wicket.
You're running, you bowl the ball
The batsman hits it, the ball flies in the air
And . . . you're under it, you catch and you win.
The crowd go wild
You wake up and it's all a dream
You have to get ready for school
Your mum is calling you
But you just want to stay in bed.

John William Clark (10)
North & South Cowton Community Primary School, Northallerton

What Could It Be?

What could the cardboard box be?
What could the cardboard box be?
It could be a boat, sailing on the sea
Or it could be a table for us to have tea
That's what the cardboard box could be.

What could the broom be?
What could the broom be?
Maybe a mast for a pirate ship
Or we could be witches on the broom for a trip
That's what the broom could be.

What could the blanket be?
What could the blanket be?
A magic carpet, flying fast
Or a skull and crossbones on a mast
That's what the blanket could be.

What could the cushions be?
What could the cushions be?
Build them up high like a tower
For a wizard with lots of power
That's what the cushions could be.

Look at all the things to do
Let's go play, just me and you.

Rachel Hannah Elphick (10)
North & South Cowton Community Primary School, Northallerton

Lemur Poem

Furry, grey, ring-tailed lemurs
Swinging through the rainforest trees
Eating bright, colourful berries
Looking after their precious babies.
Lemurs hopping, playing with their friends
Then it's time to go to bed.
So up they go into the trees
To cuddle up and go to sleep.
Waking up bright and early
Yawning as they go
Jumping to the forest floor
They start to run and play once more.

Carl Hughes (11)
North & South Cowton Community Primary School, Northallerton

Blue Tits

My little friends fluttering by
How I wish I could be with them
Up in the big blue sky.
It's a wonderful life skimming the air
With colourful feathers on fragile wings.
Hanging upside-down, eating the seeds
Flies away and happily sings.

Jack Walmsley (10)
North & South Cowton Community Primary School, Northallerton

What Am I?

Spotty fur
Yellow and black
Live in the jungle
Sleek and long
Very fast
Sharp teeth
Pointed ears
What am I?

Alice Burnett (9)
Norton Primary School, Norton

Brothers

Brothers don't care
Brothers try to put something in your ear
Brothers don't share
Brothers try to throw you off a pier
Brothers aren't smart
Brothers pull the head off your favourite teddy bear
Brothers don't listen in art
Did I mention they don't like to play truth or dare?

Rebecca Craggs (9)
Norton Primary School, Norton

What Am I?

White and cold
Soft and flaky
Glistening and patterned
Fun and slippery
What am I?

Amy Walker (9)
Norton Primary School, Norton

Older Brothers

Older brothers can get on your nerves
They are extremely annoying
But I am sure they love us
Their little sisters
Even if their way of saying it is,
'You smell!'
They still love us!

Lydia Watson (9)
Norton Primary School, Norton

Waking Up

Waking up, rise and shine
Clambering out of bed
Pulling up my socks
Jumper over head
Sliding on the rest of my clothes
Saying to myself, 'It's not time to doze!'

Brushing my teeth
Combing my hair
Eating my toast
Crumbs everywhere.

Watching the clock
It's time to go
Need to speed up
No time to slow.

It's ten to nine
We're at the school gates
I'm ready to learn
Yes
I can play with my mates!

Jasmin Abel (8)
Our Lady Of The Rosary RC Primary School, Manchester

Kennings

Floor burner
Record breaker
Tension waiting
Speedy racer
Gold toucher
Thunder Bolt
Fastest ever
Rapid runner
100m ripper
Speed grinder
Fast
(Usain Bolt)

Big boot
Goal scorer
Penalty taker
Free-kick grinder
Cross whipper
Throw in chucker
Wing runner
Stylish deliverer
Skill shower
Strong tackler
Safe hands
Powerful shoulder
Winner
(Footballer).

Jamie Greenan (10)
Our Lady Of The Rosary RC Primary School, Manchester

Nature Poem

Clouds floated across the shiny blue sky
They peered over the square block houses
Planting minute snowflakes on orange rooftops
She giggled as she drifted slowly into the distance.

Hungrily the sea crunched the golden sand
Lovely patterned shells tanned in the punishing sun
Boasting, the waterfall poured tears
Onto remote islands.

Branches argued as leaves drifted
Dancing to the ground
Bored poppies clambered under a tree for shade
Watching attentively as the green grass grew.

Hills played 'Pile On' with mountains
Streams edged their way through the game gleefully
Trying not to disturb the boasting waterfall.

Hail pelted down, pushing the wind aside
Significant chunks of ice crashed everything in its path
Tearing away at the splintered earth beneath it.

The jovial moon shyly peeked at the stars
Waltzing across the midnight velvet sky
He scored them and slowly went to sleep
Shrugging daylight from his weary shoulders.

Ciera McManamon (10)
Our Lady Of The Rosary RC Primary School, Manchester

This Hand

This hand loves to play on the computer
This hand dreams of being a builder when I am older
This hand remembers holding a snake
This hand wants to drive a Lamborghini.

Senan Geary (10)
Our Lady Of The Rosary RC Primary School, Manchester

Nature Poem

Polished stars glistening above the silent Earth
Hovering over a beautiful, royal-blue sea
The dark sky settling, as they readily illuminate
Their gorgeous, golden light, for all to see.

Cliffs proudly standing triumphantly
The sea crashing onto its legs, trying to knock them over
Only to be completely demolished
As its attempts to break its iron will are dashed.

Fields, open land, an amazing sight of green pastures,
A heaven unto all who wish to venture
To awe at the magnificent, open, desolate land
Of the Earth, showing its most proudest achievement.

Streams, reflecting the sweltering sun
Reaching a point of a wide river
Flamboyantly dancing, soon turning south
Into the majestic sea
Evolving into a surfer's awesome wave.

Gregory Francis Burke (11)
Our Lady Of The Rosary RC Primary School, Manchester

School

Monday morning, rise and shine
I can look forward to a really good time.
We jump in the car and off we go
We arrive at school where there is still some snow.
The hill is big, so we run up the side
We reach the top and down we slide.
The bell rings and we go to class
We start the lessons with English and maths.
I can't wait for the end of the day
So I can race out and continue to play.

Helena Colling (8)
Our Lady Of The Rosary RC Primary School, Manchester

Nature Poem

Treacherously the silver wind howled
Blowing the shining sun out of sight
Angry thunder argues with groaning gales
Screaming, the sea urged them to stop.

The cooling night awoke sleepily
Reflecting on the inky-blue sea
Shrugging daylight off its shoulders
Whilst the ravenous ocean munched on the crispy sea.

Barbarous branches twirled and turned
Flicking passers-by from the dark, grumbling valley
Oak trees shook their leaves vigorously
Whistling into the angry wind.

Silently the grassy hills towered
Over the quivering village
Stormy clouds wept tears of frustration
Splintering rain poured
Breaking silently on the peak of the mountains.

Matthew Petrykowski (11)
Our Lady Of The Rosary RC Primary School, Manchester

The Sea

He was awoken by the shining moon
His eyes glared at the light
Catapulting himself onto the rocks
His temper as fierce as lightning.

Strong hands grasping on the waves
Demolishing the bellowing vessels
Unleashing his mighty roar
His thunderous anger made them cry.

Ryan O'Brien (9)
Our Lady Of The Rosary RC Primary School, Manchester

Dancing Bears

In Bruin's weeping eyes
The children could sense regret
What they saw was very cruel
And something they'd not forget.

Bruin hung his head in shame
The keeper put the chain and bar in the case
They walked away with no cheer
As tears dripped down the poor bear's face.

As the keeper counted the money
The children sobbed head in hand
Bruin dreamed of a bright new future
Living with his family in a foreign land.

Gabrielle Lomas (10)
Our Lady Of The Rosary RC Primary School, Manchester

Kennings

Accident maker
Earth stomper
Noise creator
Huge waves maker
Windy swirler
Rock spewer
Shaking creator
Deafening maker
Earth cracker
Flying creator
Terrifier
Earthquake.

Matthew Hartley (9)
Our Lady Of The Rosary RC Primary School, Manchester

Nature's Power

On the golden, crisp sand
The shells with their magnificent patterns
Tanned in the punishing sun
With a gentle breeze.

The waterfall with its marvellous roar
Crashed on the rocky peaks
The wind with her invisible appearance
Whistled through the trees
After the breeze through a field of green.

The moon beams over the flowery meadows
In a calm peaceful night.

George Lowe (10)
Our Lady Of The Rosary RC Primary School, Manchester

Hurricane

A land basher
A plate smasher
A mess maker
An animal shaker
A leaf blower
An anger shower
A satellite crasher
A people killer
A house turner
A wind whirler
Terrifier.

Kate Scanlon (10)
Our Lady Of The Rosary RC Primary School, Manchester

Out And About

I went to the park and guess what was there?
Lovely flowers and green grass everywhere.

I went to the zoo and what happened there?
I saw a lion prowl into its lair.

I paddled in the sea and as I did so
A fish swam past and tickled my toe.

I went to a restaurant to eat chips and fish
This turned out to be an extraordinary dish.

I actually recognised the fish!

Molly Kelly (9)
Our Lady Of The Rosary RC Primary School, Manchester

Nature Poem

Exuberantly, glistening like an orb
The sparkling moon beamed down on the small stars
As it began to descend
Nonchalantly the clouds meandered across
The otherwise empty sky
Defenceless shells were gobbled up by
The treacherous tide
Jagged rocks squashed innocent crabs.

Aaron Rogerson (10)
Our Lady Of The Rosary RC Primary School, Manchester

I Stood In A Room

I stood in a room full of red creatures
That painted black skulls on the wall.

I stood in a room full of terror
That melted the sun.

I stood in a room full of death
With dark arrows hitting the shadows
Turning them into skeletons.

Arron Ennis (9)
Our Lady Of The Rosary RC Primary School, Manchester

Nature Poem

Flamboyant waterfalls flounced
Boasting and chattering to the colossal mountain
Shattering its peace
Grumbling, the rocks frowned, flinching at the interruption.

Wind howled
Through the long, spindly fingers of a solid oak tree
Rain splintered the ground, like bullets from a gun.

Charlie Samuel Brett (10)
Our Lady Of The Rosary RC Primary School, Manchester

I Stood In A Room

I stood in a room full of happiness
And my eyes felt as if they were sparkling
I stood in a room full of laughter
As I saw the golden sunshine through the window
I stood in a room full of courage
As bravery filled it.

Roberta Leigh (10)
Our Lady Of The Rosary RC Primary School, Manchester

My Sister

My sister is an alien who lives inside my house
She's always doing wacky things
She jumps and dances and she sings
She even keeps a pet woodlouse.

My sister is a hamster, she comes alive at night
She's always doing wacky things
She jumps and dances and she sings
She turns into a hairy thing and gives us such a fright.

My sister is a cactus; she gives me such a spike
She's always doing wacky things
She jumps and dances and she sings
She turns into a hairy thing
We have to shave her all day long
And water her all night.

My sister is a vampire who sucks up all our blood
She's always doing wacky things
She jumps and dances and she sings
She turns into a hairy thing
We have to shave her all day long
She really has a terrible pong
And she even eats mud!

I love my sister!

Megan Louisa James (10)
Pannal Primary School, Harrogate

Gymnast

Tumble and tumble, finish with a flick
I speed across the floor incredibly quick
Jumping and twisting on the bouncy floor
My heart pumping loudly as I push myself more.

Now on the bar as I fly through the air
Round and round with the wind in my hair
Like a kite in the sky on a windy day
I'm up and I'm down but my hands never stray.

I'm a tightrope walker, the beam is so thin
I jump, I leap, I flick, I spin
I try not to wobble or tremble with fear
As I try to forget and make my mind clear.

I'm running now like a lightning bolt
I charge down the track and I hit the vault
I'm twisting and turning, my mind has gone numb
Just land on your feet and not on your bum!

At last, it's all over, my mum smiling with pride
I've done all I can, now the judges decide
Who gets a medal and who gets what score
Then it's back to the classroom to practise some more.

Jessica London (9)
Pannal Primary School, Harrogate

Kiki

The ground shook, the windows smashed
The house was falling on me and I am trapped
I know I won't be able to get out on time
To get any food or water.

Here under rubble and ground
But no one's saving me, I am not found
With my sister cuddling me
And my decaying brothers surrounding me
But Mummy will come, I have faith in her!

I hear them walking around me
They are trying and trying to find me
With darkness surrounding me and that's all
I call my mum, I call and I call
But Mummy will come, I have faith in her.

I am out and I am free,
My mummy and daddy have found me
I am with my family and that's all that matters
Still my parents have found me
Mummy has come, I knew it!

Emily Hunter (9)
Pannal Primary School, Harrogate

Christmas

The computer screen blinking rapidly at the act of the virus on
Christmas Eve
When you are trying to order a last minute Christmas present
So it will arrive unexpectedly
Everybody sitting by the fire getting warm and cosy
Wrapped in their quilts, watching the snow falling violently
All the flashing decorations are making all the family dizzy
Whilst watching 'Dancing On Ice'.

Archie Griffiths (10)
Pannal Primary School, Harrogate

Live The Dream

Have you wondered how it might
Suddenly turn from day to night?
You love playing in the sun
And in the dark it can be fun!
Until you get that dreadful call,
You can't stay up
You're still too small.
So you have a bath,
Go to bed,
But there is something in your head.
A rock star strutting down the stage,
Picture splashed across the front page.
Striking the winner in the cup,
Man United sign me up.
Slogging a century in the Ashes,
I'll bowl until that wicket crashes.
Have you wondered how you might
Live the dream through the night?

Will Bennett (10)
Pannal Primary School, Harrogate

Firework Acrostic Poem

F ire sticks shoot through billowing black
I ce creamy sparkles tumble and crack
R ed carnations whistle and spin
E veryone cheers as the fireworks begin
W ood piled high is eaten by flames
O n top, Guy Fawkes is roasted again
R ockets return, blackened to ash
K aleidoscope colours collide and clash
S omewhere a screech and somewhere a crash.

Madeleine Jonsen (10)
Pannal Primary School, Harrogate

Monster

It started with a bump in the night
At first it gave me quite a fright
A loud *thud, pow, bang, crash, thump*
I thought it was my brother's trump
There were shadows on the wall
Big, scary and tall
I thought I saw glaring red eyes under my bed . . .
'Don't be so silly,' my mother once said
No one would visit - no one would sleep
This thing was giving everyone the creeps
The doors were starting to slam
They wouldn't open, like a lid on jam
One last thing did it for me . . .
I couldn't believe my eyes . . . what did I see?
I painted a picture in my mind of a huge hairy yeti
Biting off my head
There was no monster -
It was my brother hiding under my bed!

Billy Thompson (10)
Pannal Primary School, Harrogate

He Was Gone!

D arkness surrounded him, closing in on him
E verlasting torture engulfed him
A gony and pain were the last things he felt as he tossed and
    writhed
T urning to me he whispered, 'May I be triumphant even in death.'
H e welcomed death as if it were an old friend
    that showed he was truly my friend.

Alice Green (10)
Pannal Primary School, Harrogate

Nightwalk

When I got lost on a walk
The icy wind howled in my ears like a raging torrent
As I splashed through muddy puddles
While the towering trees whispered thoughts of despair.

When I got lost on a walk
The stars twinkled slyly like eyes of hyenas
As I shone the torch at the worn map
While the mouth of darkness wrapped tightly around me.

When I got lost on a walk
The trees crowded in around me like a starving lion ready for the kill
As I realised I'd hit a dead end
When minutes later reassuring lights glowed in the distance
That led me back home.

Naomi Davies (10)
Pannal Primary School, Harrogate

A Mermaid's Secret

Vain as summer
Admiring every bit of themselves in a golden mirror
Beautiful as spring
Their golden hair whipping around in the breeze
And their ruby-red lips
Their tongue is sweet with dangerous songs
Leading sailors and ships to their deaths
Their mind is full of prophecy
Telling the future with their double-sided minds
Their grace in the water
Speeding through the crystal water
We know little of these creatures
However, I know the secret of the mermaid.

Cammryn Reagan (10)
Pannal Primary School, Harrogate

The Bedroom

My hair played gently with my fingers
The book danced gracefully on the bookshelf
My eyes glowed when the sunshine
Came through my bedroom window
The alarm clock chatted peacefully
To the beautiful music playing softly
The juicy orange elbowed the chocolate angrily
As they waited calmly in the drawer
The bed's arms held me tight
While I lay there feeling heavenly
The curtains moved swiftly side to side
While the wind came in quickly.

Megan Gough (10)
Pannal Primary School, Harrogate

Kennings

Steady plodder
Grass grazer
Cud chewer
Methane producer
Milk supplier
Calf deliverer
Mega mooer.

Megan Homburg (10)
Pannal Primary School, Harrogate

The Twins

I have a twin
She likes to win
When we play together.

We sit in bed
Going red
When we laugh together.

We like to sing
Wearing bling
When we sing together.

We'll have our lives
Doing high fives
When we grow up together.

Abigail Morris (9)
St John's CE Primary School, Great Harwood

My Horse

His name is Shandiss
Runs round and round
In a dirty stable
We spend more than a pound.

Mucking out the stable
Feeding him his hay
Grooming him takes ages
He always wants to play.

Riding him in the arena
Galloping in the field
The shows are not long off
He's always hurting my heels.

Olivia Shepherd
St John's CE Primary School, Great Harwood

Me And My Horse Poem

H appiest times
O K riding
R acing horse
S pecial horse
E xcellent horse

R esting horse
I nteresting horse
D ozy horse
I ntelligent horse
N ice horse
G alloping horse.

Shannon Dewale
St John's CE Primary School, Great Harwood

The Football Poem

Football is a great sport
They always give it a lot of thought
Me and you can play the game
We will never give it a lot of shame

Don't be shy
We can do it if we try
We can run, we can kick
Come on again, we aren't thick.

Come on you guys!

Lauren McCann (9)
St John's CE Primary School, Great Harwood

Mum And Dad

M um is excellent
U nreal
M ad

A ngry
N ice
D aft duck

D ad is brilliant
A bsolutely fantastic
D elightful Dad.

Brandon Baron (9)
St John's CE Primary School, Great Harwood

My Holiday

M ilkshakes are delicious
Y ou can swim in the pools

H ot and sunny on the beach
O h I
L ove playing in the sun
I ce cream is super cold
D isco, lots of bright lights
A lways wear suncream
Y ou have to wear a fantastic hat.

Declan Youds (10)
St John's CE Primary School, Great Harwood

Brownies

B rown Owl, leaders
R unning games
O utside games in summer
W riting about ourselves
N ice friends
I nteresting games
E ating lunch
S inging songs.

Lucie Lyne (10)
St John's CE Primary School, Great Harwood

Football

Football
Score goals
Look before passing
Run fast and dodge
Tackle the teams
Be careful
Win.

Arbab Hussain
St John's CE Primary School, Great Harwood

Swimming Is Fun!

Swimming
Waves high
Inflatables are good
Having a great time
Splashing in the water
Dive deep
Fun!

Lewis Taylor (9)
St John's CE Primary School, Great Harwood

Football

Foot
Dribbles, fast,
Speeding, tackling, dodging,
Painful, goals, angry, hard,
Bulging, hurting, netting,
Big, solid,
Ball.

Kyle Tibbett (9)
St John's CE Primary School, Great Harwood

Me And My Baby Sister, Heidi

Me
Nice, kind
Helping, behaving, loving,
Silly, tidy, funny, cute,
Sleeping, dribbling, crying,
Baby sister
Heidi.

Olivia Stewart (10)
St John's CE Primary School, Great Harwood

Fish

F ishing is the best
I like catching mackerel
S hadows of fish
H appy time fishing
I kiss what I catch
N etting my catch
G ood fish to eat.

Phillip Marsay (9)
St John's CE Primary School, Great Harwood

Me And My Best Friend

We like to sing
We like to dance
We like to play every day and night

We love sleepovers
We love to be together
And we *love* to be best friends.

Sophie Talbot (9)
St John's CE Primary School, Great Harwood

My Sister

S ometimes cute
I s a goody-two-shoes
S illy most of the time
T reats me best
E very way she helps me
R ough at times.

Ella Morris (9)
St John's CE Primary School, Great Harwood

Big Eating

1, 2, 3, 4, 5
I roasted my dog alive
6, 7, 8, 9, 10
I spat him out again
10, 11, 12, 13
Now I'll try it again!

Duncan Steele (8)
St John's CE Primary School, Great Harwood

Superpowers

'I have a superpower, Miss,' I said
And she said, 'Be quiet or it's off to the head!'
Next minute I put up my hand to say,
'Miss, come out to see me flying at play!'

She said, 'Oh, be quiet Charlie.'
And I said, 'All right, Mrs Smarty.'
And she said, 'How dare you, Charlie Bay?
Your name is on the board for the rest of the day.'

A few days later when I was taking a walk,
I saw Miss being stolen by a great big hawk.
I thought to myself, *Oh dear, oh dear*
Miss, you've got into quite a lot of trouble here.

I thought, *should I save her or should I not?*
If I did I'd get money, of that, quite a lot.
Then I thought, *OK, I'll have to make a decision.*
It was quite hard to do this in my position.

So, what was better, one or two?
Saving her life or watching, 'Where are we going to?'
Well, getting prizes is very good
So I'll go for saving the lady in the wood.

So up I flew and pinched our old friend, Hawk,
Straight away he turned with a great big squawk
And dropped her to plummet to the ground,
So I flew down at the speed of sound!

I grabbed her by her long thick hair
And placed her on a garden chair.
Next day she said, 'I won't doubt you again.'
And gave me a mark of ten out of ten!

Rebecca Wurr (10)
St John's RC Primary School, Chorlton

When I Look At Creation

When I look at creation, I see the waves
Rolling to the shore,
The trees swaying in the breeze
And the animals crawling across the land.

When I look at creation, I see the dark night sky
Spreading itself across the Earth.
I see the sun rise amongst the clouds,
Making everyone smile.

When I look at creation, I see flowers full of life
Springing up from the damp, moist soil.
I see the death of a crispy leaf
Floating gently to the ground.

When I look at creation, I see birds
Soaring through the clear blue sky.
I see a determined turtle,
Plodding across the land.

When I look at creation, I see the fish
Dancing beneath the waves,
As a clumsy octopus
Clutches to a slippery rock.

When I look at creation, I see intelligent people
Caring for God's world,
A weeping baby in the loving arms of its mother,
I see a family of friendship in the world,
When I look at creation, I see a wonderful place.

Isobel Priest (10)
St John's RC Primary School, Chorlton

Man City

When I'm at a City match, I jump around and scream,
But when I'm sitting in my house, I quietly eat ice cream.
My favourite player is Tevez, he's really, really good,
He even pushed Wayne Rooney into a pile of mud!

When City beat United, I was sure we'd start anew
But then my dreams were shattered when Wayne Rooney scored
two.
We had players injured, things were looking bleak,
Wayne Bridge got an injury so our defence was really weak.

I love to go to City matches, it makes me really glad,
But when we leather United, their fans go extremely mad.
When City sing their songs, they're as loud as they can be,
40,000 singing, that's not including me.

But now our cup run is over, it really is a pity,
But I'll be coming next week because I love supporting City.
I was born a City fan, you should know that's true,
Because the blood in my body is not red, it's blue.

City score a lot of goals,
They're so hard, they make some holes.
My poem now is almost done,
Writing this poem was a lot of fun.

City is a great team
And that's why I chose them for my theme.
I'm tired now, I'm going to bed,
So just remember, I'm not a red!

Niall Manford (10)
St John's RC Primary School, Chorlton

The Wind And The Sun

The wind is howling through the trees
Terrible tempests on a breeze;
Sun beaming down, shining bright
Amazing strength, bright, bright light.

One winter's morn Wind said to Sun,
'Come with me and have some fun -
The cheerful children in the park
I'll make them take off their scarves.'

The wind blew harder than ever before,
He wailed and howled till he couldn't anymore.
When he struck the frosty park
The cold children put on a scarf.

Then Sun said, 'Can I have a go?'
But didn't puff and didn't blow,
Instead he shone a dazzling white
Hotter and hotter, extremely bright.

Symmetrical patterns made of ice
Swirls and whirls of shiny white,
Sun soon melted them with light
And still shone very bright.

The children's scarves were off in a flash,
Away for a drink and sunglasses they dashed.
'Nice hot weather for everyone
And I took off their scarves,' beamed Sun.

Lucy Chadwick (10)
St John's RC Primary School, Chorlton

God's Creation

God has a wonderful imagination
Because He made all of creation
He made everything all colourful
Just to make the world so, so beautiful
It's God creation.

I love to see the birds in the sky
I like seeing all of them fly
They all fly to a great height
Where all you can see is a blanket of white
That is God's creation.

But what makes me feel sick and green
Is watching the world being so mean
I love all the places in the world:
Africa, Asia, Europe and America.

God made the sea
And it's great enjoyment for me
If I could go to Australia, this would be my wish
To go to the barrier reef and look at God's fish
I like it in the morning when it's all light
But I hate it at night-time when it's not so bright
This is God's creation.

Alejandro Curry-Lujan (10)
St John's RC Primary School, Chorlton

Sports

Football is fun,
Especially when you've won.
Cricket is great
When you hit it straight.
Swimming is cool
When you are in the pool.

Zak Smith (9)
St John's RC Primary School, Chorlton

Weeks And Months Teach Me

Weeks and months teach me to always dream
However, it may never come true
But that's the best way to live life through.

Weeks and months teach me to dream so high
Never give up and always try
Never let go or say goodbye.

Weeks and months teach me that when there is darkness
For sure, dawn is the next
And when everything is so tiring
For sure, there will be time to rest.

Weeks and months teach me to always care for a friend
Always be true and never pretend
Always love with no end
And the broken hearts will mend.

Weeks and months teach me never to feel hate
Always be confident and never hesitate
Always believe in fate.

Weeks and months teach me
The past I must forget
And nothing needs my regret.

Liam Atanga (10)
St John's RC Primary School, Chorlton

Winter And Snow

W ild snow gently drifts down from the sky
 I enjoy every second of freedom
N ext day I dream to sled
 T o the highest and biggest mountains
E ven though the snow will melt and go
R acing and playing for now, I love the snow.

John-Joe Merritt (10)
St John's RC Primary School, Chorlton

Football

Football, football, I score goals
Everyone reckons I'm as good as Paul Scholes
Football, football, I like Ryan Giggs
Not many people know he's good at Irish jigs.

Football, football, I met John O'Shea
He has a really good friend called Ray
Football, football, I run down the wing
All the fans cheer and sing.

Football, football, I like to hit the ball with power
Football training only goes on for one hour
Football, football, I like to celebrate
I also like to cheer on my mates.

Football, football, I'm number seven
I got offered number eleven
Football, football, sometimes I'm a goalie
At the end of the game I do a roly poly.

Football, football, City are bad
When they lose they are all sad
Football, football, Man U fans cheer
Most of the adults have a pint of beer.

Jacob Burke (9)
St John's RC Primary School, Chorlton

Weather

Sun shines, rain falls,
Snow comes, wind calls
Weather, weather, good and bad
Weather can make you feel happy and sad.

Shannon Debotte (10)
St John's RC Primary School, Chorlton

Tall And Towering Teacher

Tall and towering teacher,
With a big and warty nose,
You scare me oh so very much,
You once even wet me with a hose.

Tall and towering teacher,
You look like you want a munch,
I'm sure if we were naughty,
You'd eat us for your lunch.

Tall and towering teacher,
Please don't gobble me up,
Don't mix me up with green gunge,
And slurp me from a cup.

Tall and towering teacher,
I'm sorry I talked in mass,
I'm sorry I didn't do my homework,
And I'm sorry I wet myself in class.

But I'll never do that again,
Promise, I really, really will,
But I'm having a day off anyway,
Even though I don't feel ill.

Niamh Grimes (10)
St John's RC Primary School, Chorlton

Different Sport

Football, football, you score goals
It's like a cherry scone
Tennis, tennis, you hit the ball, bat to bat
And wear a funky yellow hat
Rugby, rugby, tackle a man
The men had a ban.

Skip, skip, as long as you can
And the most skips wins
Then you can stay in
Cricket, cricket, hit the ball as far as you can
And try and get lots of runs
And you have lots of fun
Athletics, athletics, running is fun
Running, running it's so much fun to run.

Hockey, hockey, the ball runs around like a mini man
And conks someone on the head with a saucepan
Judo, judo, doing cool moves
And give it a cool groove
Skiing, skiing, down the snowy hill
As I am taking a pill.

Tia McHale (9)
St John's RC Primary School, Chorlton

The Haunted House!

If you dare enter this room,
You will hear a *bim-bam-boom!*
A ghost walks past with vile eyes,
And there a dead mummy lies.

The door handles pull your hair and eat it,
You tell them to go away, 'Beat it!'

All the portraits come out for real,
And eat you with their Sunday meal,
They scare you so you jump
And hit you so you get a lump.

They gang up and scare you,
Then they touch you and shout, 'Boo!'
Beware of the little rats
And the baby kitty kats.

You feel like a baby mouse,
So don't go in the haunted house!

Sam Cowan (10)
St John's RC Primary School, Chorlton

Football, Football

Football, football, what do you say?
I am good at football
I score a lot of goals
I am nearly as good as Paul Scholes.

I run down the wing as fast as Wayne Rooney
But I don't have good shots
It feels like I have chickenpox
But I always mess about
Like in the classroom
When I get shouted at.

Giovanni Salmon (10)
St John's RC Primary School, Chorlton

Tilly And Milly

There once was a young girl called Tilly,
Who had a best friend called Milly.
They went down to the planet garden and saw a plant
That had lots of creepy ants.

The next day they made a yummy cake,
They both said, 'Keep an eye on it, someone could take our cake.'
They made chocolate cake, they said it was yummy
Their mums even said it was yummy in their tummies.

On the third day Tilly and Milly went to swim
With their best friend, Jim
They went to play
In the middle of May.

On the fourth day Tilly and Milly were at a party
They had a pack of sweets, Smarties
They like meeting new people at shops
But they like to mop.

Olivia Cravagan (9)
St John's RC Primary School, Chorlton

Mummy I Love . . .

M ummy, I love chocolate cookies
U p and down my belly goes
M ummy, Mummy, I love the bookies
M ummy, Mummy, I've got a big tummy
Y ummy, yummy, says my tummy

I love chocolate, especially chocolate chips

L ovely melting buns
O ver on the table lies a melting chocolate cake
V olcanoes bursting in my mouth as I eat tons and tons
E veryone in my class made me a cake but it was fake!

Ciaran Poole (9)
St John's RC Primary School, Chorlton

Down Where The Animals Go

Down in the jungle the lion prowls
Down in the jungle the tiger growls
Down in the jungle the birds all sing
Down in the jungle the monkeys swing.

Down at the farm the cow goes *moo*
Down at the farm the chicken goes *cock-a-doodle-doo*
Down at the farm the pig trots around
Down at the farm the horse has the loudest sound.

Down in the forest the eagles fly
Down in the forest the bears pass by
Down in the forest the mice squeak
Down in the forest the woodpecker pecks his beak.

Under the sea the fish goes *flap*
Under the sea the crab goes *snap*
Under the sea the shark blows bubbles
Under the sea the dolphin gives you cuddles.

Emma De Paola (9)
St John's RC Primary School, Chorlton

A Poem By Owen

As I wiped the sweat off my forehead,
I wished I had stayed longer in bed.
My head was hurting, I couldn't remember last night,
When the ball came near, I received a sudden fright.
Fergie was mad as well as the whole team,
But I couldn't see anything except the trophy gleam.

Suddenly a rush of determination pushed me on,
I even banged Terry into a sign reading *Eon,*
I dribbled past Lampard (he thought I was a looney)
But guess who scored the goal? Wide-faced Rooney!

Frankie Finan (10)
St John's RC Primary School, Chorlton

Fish!

Swimming swiftly through the sea,
Red, gold and orange, what could it be?
Its black beady eyes watch as I pass,
So I kick my legs and go by fast.

As I pass I spot a light,
It's a pearl covered in white.
I go down to pick it up,
Then all of a sudden something bites my foot.

Wonderful fish all around,
Some up high and some on the ground.
The sharks come past, all dark and grey,
They're swimming around looking for their prey.

It's time to go now from the sea
And when I get out I get stung by a bee.
I've had a great day,
On the 9th of May.

Erin Norcross (9)
St John's RC Primary School, Chorlton

The Swamp

In the swamp it's dark and damp
You would usually bump into a tramp
If you're not careful you'll fall in the marsh
And trust me, it's sticky and harsh
The trees look like they're slowly moving
But it's just a big illusion
And if you decide to go too far in
You will be put in the bin
By spooky goblins here and there
So run, don't let your life fade in despair.

James Fraser (9)
St John's RC Primary School, Chorlton

81

My Monster Mum

When my mum gets angry,
She grows a long green tail,
I get so scared and frightened,
It makes me feel all frail.

Her ears grow huge and pointy,
Her eyes begin to swell,
When I try to calm her down,
All she does is yell.

I wish I was a mini mouse,
As small as can be,
So I could hide in tiny cracks,
Where she could not see me.

How can I tame this wild beast?
I'm in a helpless muddle,
I'll make her a lovely cup of tea,
And give her a great big cuddle.

Maisie Metcalfe-Chung (10)
St John's RC Primary School, Chorlton

The Shoe

She walks around the street with one shoe
Everyone points and stares and says, 'It's blue.'
She wears odd socks, but no one cares
Because she's got chickenpox everywhere.

She's always tripping over and she gets mud all over
She has a hat to keep her warm and she has a cat
She has no coat but she would like a boat
She hops all around on the dirty, filthy ground.

Martikka Kaur (10)
St John's RC Primary School, Chorlton

England

England, England, we're so good
We invented a type of hood
We invented the phone, yes
England really is the best!

We invented football, cool
Now it is played at our school
Manchester, Manchester, we love you
For inventing the Internet, phew.

England, England, helping Haiti
England, England, for making my matey
England, England, is so small
But it helps many countries in a brawl.

England, England, we're so good
We invented a type of hood
We invented the phone, yes
England really is the best!

James Brennan (9)
St John's RC Primary School, Chorlton

Sports

Football, football, it is fun
Especially when you have just won
Cricket, cricket, it is great
Especially when you hit it straight
Swimming, swimming, it is cool
When you are playing in the pool
Sports, sports, they are good for you
Which ones do you like to do?

Henry Holt (9)
St John's RC Primary School, Chorlton

The Leprechaun

In Ireland along the sunny banks,
Sits a little leprechaun in his dark green pants.
In his little light green hat,
He sits on his black and white striped mat.

Every day he plays hurling,
With his friends Keenan, Connor and Merlin.
They laugh and play every day,
In the warmth of May.

His name is Evan,
He is aged seven.
In his little green hat,
On his black and white mat.

In Ireland along the sunny banks,
Sits a little leprechaun in his dark green pants.
In his little light green hat,
He sits on his black and white mat.

Niamh Gorman (9)
St John's RC Primary School, Chorlton

Homework

Miss says, 'Where's your homework?'
'Err, at home.'
'Why is it at home?'
'Because I died last night and came back to life Miss.'
So at break I was running
And fell and pulled my teacher's pants down
She was blushing bright red
And she send me to the head.

Matthew Owen (10)
St John's RC Primary School, Chorlton

Every Night

The night spreads itself along the face of the Earth,
Before night gives way to a day's birth.
That's when the animals come out
Like bats and hedgehogs with their little snouts.
Night is when the Earth goes to sleep,
Nobody makes a little peep,
Except for the animals that are nocturnal
And my rowdy neighbour the Colonel!
He shouts and screams
The poor street never gets sweet dreams.
Then I say, 'Enough's enough!
It's about time I got tough.'
And as I creep down the stairs,
Keeping hold of my two teddy bears
I go to his door but all I hear is a loud snore
I think, *what a relief*
My visit was very brief.

Calum Conner Jones (10)
St John's RC Primary School, Chorlton

Brothers

B rothers, brothers, they always lie
R unning from the room, they will always deny
O f all the trouble that they cause
T his would not lead to a round of applause
H aving a brother isn't really so bad
E very now and then if I'm feeling sad
R ay and Ben will do something daft
S o both of my brothers will make me laugh.

Jack Sheehan (10)
St John's RC Primary School, Chorlton

The Little Boat

A little boat
Floating by
A shadow in the moonlit sky

Full of dreams
And wonders too
Then one day it'll come to you

Rocking gently
To and fro
Waving to people as it goes

Ruby-red
Amazing bright blue
We'll stop by, just for you

Floating away
Into your dreams
When you wake up, it's nothing like it seems.

Orla Felcey (9)
St John's RC Primary School, Chorlton

Football

The goal's shot
Scare the lot
As play goes on
Rooney follows on

Ronaldhino's skill
Jumps past the bill
The league is won
As goals go on

Ronaldo scores goals
To put United through
To three goals

Free kicks fly in
From the lash of the shin
The goal's shot
Scared the lot.

Sam Connolly (9)
St John's RC Primary School, Chorlton

The Snow

Today it snowed
It was so cold
The snow was white
It was so bright
So I just might
Go out and play all night
When the snow is out at night
The moon and stars shine so bright
All the kids like the snow
So they can slip and slide as they go
When the snow starts to defrost
Home goes Jack Frost.

Kian O'Grady (10)
St John's RC Primary School, Chorlton

God's Creation

God made the trees that blow in the wind
God made the flowers that open in spring
God made the birds flying up above
God made them all with His special love
God made the grass that was so very green
God made the rain that washes everything clean
God made the snow that is fluffy and white
God made the sun that shines so bright
God made the mountains, so high, so tall
God made the insects, so tiny, so small
God made the fish that swim in the sea
God made these things for you and for me
God gave me a loving family
God gave me these things to live happily
God gave me the greatest gift He could
God gave me His warm and gentle love.

Jamie Kukielka (10)
St John's RC Primary School, Chorlton

Snow

Snow, snow, everywhere
It's a shame it doesn't grow
Icy patches down below
Cold winds blow.

Everybody is tucked up
Aww, where are all the ducks?
All animals are hibernating
No one's playing football.

Building snowmen
Making a den
it's so much fun!

John Purcell (9)
St John's RC Primary School, Chorlton

Factory Working

Are you willing to apply for a job
At Mark and Deck's Mardy Mob?
Do you know when something's about to boom
When you're working at the contained fume?
Make sure you don't sniff the gloop
Or it may smell like a vat of poop.
Don't forget to get your tour
'Cause after that there's help no more.
In your locker you'll find a protective suit
But wherever you look you won't find a boot.
If you get promoted you can start managing
Get more payment and less working.
Everywhere machinery is whizzing
Just listen to those gas tanks hissing.
Check in at the reception desk
And aim to be the very best!

Joseph Basic (10)
St John's RC Primary School, Chorlton

3.30PM

3.30pm is the best time of the day,
The sweet feeling inside is something you can't describe,
When I step outside the feeling of excitement gives me butterflies,
I love to see the joy in my parents' faces as we leave the school grounds,
My feeling is high, the excitement I get you just can't forget,
I arrive home at four, knocking on my door,
I'm greeted by my dog, excited even more.
My mum makes my dinner which makes my belly rumble,
I am happy and humble when my dad makes apple crumble,
Then I watch TV for an hour
And I decide to take a shower.
When I take too long my mum starts singing that same old song,
'Come on out of the shower, you've been in there for an hour.'
I dry myself off and get ready for bed
My dad reads my glorious Secret Seven stories.

Kofi Biney (10)
St John's RC Primary School, Chorlton

The Lion

The lion, so fierce, so big, so scary,
All of his body, his tail so hairy.
The lion will show off his power and might,
By doing what he loves best, to roar and to fight.

The lion, at night will go for a prowl,
And scare all the animals with his low, hungry growl.
The lion with his claws will rip any meat
And then, after that, will lie in the midsummer heat.

The lion, with flies flying around that golden mane of his,
Making the inside of him bubble and fizz.
The lion, galloping across the vast, open plain
And in the wind blowing is every hair of his soft, golden mane.

The lion, your eyes so beautiful and brown,
This is why you deserve the king's mighty crown.

Amelia Boon (10)
St John's RC Primary School, Chorlton

Dancing

Dancing, prancing in the air
Swaying, flicking soft, silky hair
Sparkly costumes in the bright lights
Twinkling like a star in the dark blue nights.

Boom, boom, pow! Let's dance, dance, dance
Boom, boom, pow! Let's thump not prance
Cool dance. *Bang, bang, bang!*
Cool clothes. *Bang, bang, bang!*

Jump, hop, skip and up
When you land there's no thump
Skip away, away, away
And then you're really OK.

Niamh Norcross (9)
St John's RC Primary School, Chorlton

The Ghost

Castle, castle, oh so high,
In thy walls the spirits lie.
Your men and women work day and night
To praise thy king and all his might.
Take up arms and you will see
Everyone is afraid of thee,
Beyond the trees your enemies wait.
Build your defences before it's too late,
If you do not, the spirits will grow,
For war brings death for friend and foe.
A messenger to speak of peace, go send,
Sign a truce and be their friend.

Trust me now king, for I must go,
Take heed of my message for I am your ghost.

Matteo Rawlinson (10)
St John's RC Primary School, Chorlton

The Knight

A long time ago there lived a knight,
Who when younger was a slave,
But in later life proved he was very brave,
He charged through the fields swinging his mighty shield
To defend the King.

He battled ogres, he battled trolls
And had them cowering in their holes.
He did not stop till his work was done
And had very little time for games and fun.

The King rewarded him with lots of treasures
With which he and his family had lots of pleasure.
He lived to the age of eighty-two and was best remembered
For the battle of Swampygoo.

Milo Crier (10)
St John's RC Primary School, Chorlton

The Shadowed Assassin

Off with the shadows of the black night he creeps,
His destination, a house where a widow weeps.
In one thrust of his hand he becomes unseen,
For he's the greatest assassin there's ever been.
He creeps upstairs to the bedroom with a bow,
Strapped to his back are some shiny steel arrows.
He pulls and releases one quickly, it strikes her head,
Slowly she droops, as she droops she falls from the soft bed.
Her lifeless body lays limp on the cold floor,
So he sprints and says no more.
Finally he reaches his followers' wet camp,
He lays down weary on the ground that is damp,
He retells the story of his dark killing,
They find the tale disturbing, yet thrilling.

Matthew Baines (10)
St John's RC Primary School, Chorlton

Playtime Is The Best!

The bell goes, it's time to play,
It's kids' favourite time of day.
Kids in the playground, playing hide-and-seek,
Meanwhile Mrs Cadoo sits on her seat.
Look around you, look at the sight,
Boys in dark blue, girls in bright white.
Look at the boys playing tiggy-bob-down,
Whilst the girls play with a little toy crown.
Kids in the playground with all their close friends,
Then someone shouts, 'Quick, it's nearly the end.'
The whistle goes to give us the sign,
In just five seconds we're all in a line,
Into the class, we're on our way,
Two more breaks till the end of the day.

Rose Wilson (10)
St John's RC Primary School, Chorlton

Football, Football

Football, football
Everyone's mad
And Man U is very bad
There is only one team for me
AC, AC, that's me.

Ronaldhino: god of skill
He's better than anyone at the skill
Goal, goal, goal!

Football, football
AC, AC, AC, that's the team
Never Man U, never City
What is football?
It is the power of the hour.

Dominic Simpkin (9)
St John's RC Primary School, Chorlton

The Captain's Ship

The captain's ship was dark and dull,
An oozie green mould sat on the hull,
The forbidding, black sails were ripped and torn,
The captain's men were as busy as bees that would swarm.

Some of the men were drowning in beer,
But when the lookout screamed, the shore was near,
The canons were firing, *bing, bang, boom!*
The villagers were yelling, 'But why, but whom?'

Their question was soon answered as the captain said,
'Come on me maties, they be gone or dead!'
The crew came sprinting out of the ship,
The villagers were in for more than a nip!

Kieran Smethurst (10)
St John's RC Primary School, Chorlton

Beyond

Dragons breathing red flames
Elves playing magic games
Goblins jumping round and round
Ogres chopping all around.

Sea monsters looming way up high
Young chicks attempting to fly
Mermaids singing wonderful tunes
The great Kraken, the size of moons.

Medusa with her snake-like hair
The Minotaur making fights unfair
Gorgons with their stony eyes
Fighting soldiers with their high-pitched cries.

George Hilton (9)
St John's RC Primary School, Chorlton

Writer's Block

I do not know what I should write,
I hope that it won't take all night.
There's so much stuff that I could do
But where to start, I have no clue.

Will it be good? Will it be bad?
Will it be funny? Will it be sad?
'What should I do?' I ask my dad
'I don't know, maybe something mad?'

I work my pencil to the core
And then I hear my parents snore.
It really is getting late,
I cry out loud, 'This poem I hate!'

'I cannot do this thing,' I said
So I closed my book and go to bed.

Daniel Campion (11)
St Mary's RC Primary School, Newcastle upon Tyne

The Ancient Greek Olympics

Bring it on.
I can taste the most terrible taste of oxen fat and blood,
But the sweaty air doesn't compare to the disgusting smell of oxen fat.

Bring it on.

Never give up.

I felt nervous to watch the end of the last race,
The athletes were so puffed out,
They felt the ground shaking below their feet.

Never give up.

I'm ready.

The festival has started and I can smell fresh bread being baked,
I can also smell blood.

I'm ready.

Let's do this.

I can hear the crowd screaming for the country they support,
I can also hear my heartbeat because I am so nervous.

Let's do this.

Give it all you've got.

I can see people running to win the race,
I can also see people's wounds from things they were doing.

Give it all you've got.

Catherine Latimer (9)
St Mary's RC Primary School, Newcastle upon Tyne

The Ancient Greek Olympics

I think I see, I think I see
Me winning that javelin event
And getting that green, silky garland
On my head
I think I see, I think I see.

I think I hear, I think I hear
People cheering on the chariot race
On day two of the Olympics
And people praying for Zeus on day one
I think I hear, I think I hear.

I think I smell, I think I smell
Horrible oxen meat, it smells so bad
But ancient Olympians like it
I think I smell, I think I smell.

I think I taste, I think I taste
That horrible oxen meat, it's not
Right for me, but the sweet taste of
A bird tweeting. That is definitely the one for me
I think I taste, I think I taste.

I think I feel, I think I feel
My arms are boxing away
And men are waiting to find out
Who's won the fight
And who's getting that garland
I think I feel, I think I feel.

Grace Brown (9)
St Mary's RC Primary School, Newcastle upon Tyne

The Ancient Greek Olympics

I can see
I can see
A big strong man running with weights
The athletes looking fierce
And also wrestling.

I can hear
I can hear
The horses' hooves slamming on the ground
The crunching of the wrestlers' opponents' bones
And the screaming of the crowd.

I can smell
I can smell
Sweat from the athletes
Blood from the wrestlers
And worst of all, fat and bones of the oxen.

I can taste
I can taste
The juice and meat of oxen
It tastes delicious
It tastes divine.

I can feel
I can feel
The ground shaking with thousands of runners
The wind blowing in my face
And the feeling of someone else's jealousy.

Emily Taylor (9)
St Mary's RC Primary School, Newcastle upon Tyne

The Ancient Greek Olympics

In Olympia I see
A sweaty man throwing a rock,
Oxen getting slaughtered,
A horse getting food,
In Olympia I see.

In Olympia I hear
A chariot getting pulled
And a warrior shouting orders,
Taunting opponents to attack,
In Olympia I hear.

In Olympia I smell
Sweating wrestlers who've just had a fight,
Oxen getting burned
And fire burning wood,
In Olympia I smell.

In Olympia I taste
Oxen meat that has been burned
And other animals too,
I can taste the victory in the air,
In Olympia I taste.

In Olympia I feel
Vibrations in the ground,
I feel the excitement in the crowd,
And I feel the horse's mane,
In Olympia I feel.

Nathan James (10)
St Mary's RC Primary School, Newcastle upon Tyne

The Ancient Greek Olympics

What a smell I smell
Olympians smell a dreadful smell
And smell of horses' manure
What a smell I smell.

What a sight I see
Mighty muscles on a man
Oxen getting sliced up
Soft sand on the land
What a sight I see.

What a sound I hear
Men trembling in fear
Swords slicing through the oxen
Crowds cheering
Feet stomping on the ground
What a sound I hear.

What a taste I taste
The sticky sweat of the men
Rotten flesh of the oxen
The nerves of the wrestlers
What a taste I taste.

What a feeling I feel
The breeze blowing slightly
Smoke of the oxen burning in my face
The nerves of the contestants
What a feeling I feel.

Jack Hodgson (9)
St Mary's RC Primary School, Newcastle upon Tyne

The Ancient Greek Olympics

Such food I tasted
The juicy inside of a lovely orange
And the chewy meat of an oxen
I tasted victory!
Such food I tasted.

Such cheering I heard
I heard the crowd chanting
Everybody cheering for different people
What a tremendous noise
Such cheering I heard.

What extraordinary sights I saw
I saw a Mexican wave zoom across the stadium
And sweat dripping down from my head
One hundred oxen being sacrificed
What extraordinary sights I saw.

What amazing things I felt
I felt the sweat running down my body
I always felt excited
I felt the gushing winds of the chariots
What amazing things I felt.

Such smells I smelt
I smelt the horrible oxen getting burnt
I smelt the sweat from all the other competitors
And smelt all of the soft fruits
Such smells I smelt.

Nathan Aspery (9)
St Mary's RC Primary School, Newcastle upon Tyne

The Ancient Greek Olympics

I think I can see
A lady falling off her chariot
And all the others laughing at her
The laughing in the crowd looks silly
I think I can see.

I think I can feel
The ground shaking underneath my feet
From the runners running their fastest
Day two is when they run
I think I can feel.

I think I can hear
The applause growing louder
For the oxen being killed on day three
And a cheer when all have some
I think I can hear.

I think I can smell
The oxen blood
The sweat from all the men
And the metal from the long-jump weights
I think I can smell.

I think I can taste
The juicy oxen meat sizzling under my tongue
The nerves in all the athletes
But also the excitement
I think I can taste.

Rebecca Hopkinson (10)
St Mary's RC Primary School, Newcastle upon Tyne

The Ancient Greek Olympics

Great Olympia holds the smells
Of oxen fat and bones and the sticky sweat of the athletes
You can smell the horse manure
But you don't really want to smell that
Great Olympia holds the smells.

Great Olympia holds the sights
Of oxen getting slaughtered, then eaten
All the events including wrestling, javelin, running, discus, jumping
And loads of more fantastic events
Great Olympia holds the sights.

Great Olympia holds the sounds
Of oxen grunting, people cheering on the athletes
I can hear the horses stamping their feet on the ground
I can hear people praying in the temple of Zeus
Great Olympia holds the sounds.

Great Olympia holds the feelings
Of when the athletes jump on to the silky sand
I can feel my legs getting worn out
I can feel the crowd's voice reflecting off my face
Great Olympia holds the feelings.

Great Olympia holds the taste
Of the meat of the oxen
And the taste of the water
And the olives from the branch
Great Olympia holds the taste.

Joseph Renner (10)
St Mary's RC Primary School, Newcastle upon Tyne

The Ancient Greek Olympics

I think I saw, I think I saw,
Men racing at the speed of light,
Women whipping their horses so they could win the crown,
Men jumping with enormous weights in their hands,
I think I saw, I think I saw.

I think I heard, I think I heard,
Oxen grunting like foghorns,
The pattering of men's feet racing towards the finish line,
Mad fans supporting their favourite,
I think I heard, I think I heard.

I think I smelled, I think I smelled,
Oxen's fat and bones,
The sweat of heroic boxers fighting with each other,
The smell of pressure in the air,
I think I smelled, I think I smelled.

I think I felt, I think I felt,
The anticipation from the crowd,
The pride of the champions when they got their crown,
Pressure on the Olympians,
I think I felt, I think I felt.

I think I tasted, I think I tasted,
The sweat from the Olympians,
Oxen meat with blood all over it,
All the anticipation from the crowd,
I think I tasted, I think I tasted.

Matthew Joyce (10)
St Mary's RC Primary School, Newcastle upon Tyne

The Ancient Greek Olympics

Great games of Olympia
The sight I saw of
Giant people
Galloping through the sand
A great big arm
With a mighty muscle
And I can see the soft sand
Great games of Olympia.

And such a sound I heard
The crowd cheering
To the contestants
And I could hear the wind
From people rushing across
The track
Great games of Olympia.

The smell I smelled
The rotten, revolting flesh
And the horrible horse manure
From the chariot races
Great games of Olympia.

I could feel the wind blowing
Through my hair
And the ground shaking madly
From the runners' steps
Great games of Olympia.

Bethany Hewitson (9)
St Mary's RC Primary School, Newcastle upon Tyne

The Ancient Greek Olympics

In the ancient Greek Olympics,
I can see someone flexing their muscles
And women entering their horses into chariot races,
In the ancient Greek Olympics.

In the ancient Greek Olympics,
I can smell the horrible smell of oxen being slaughtered,
The lovely smell of food all around me,
I can almost smell the sweat of the warriors,
In the ancient Greek Olympics.

In the ancient Greek Olympics,
I can taste the dirt on the ground as I'm pushed over,
I can taste the delicious meat as it touches my tongue,
I can taste the excitement in the air,
In the ancient Greek Olympics.

In the ancient Greek Olympics,
I can hear the screams of the oxen and the applause of the crowd
As the winners get their awards,
I can hear the champions cheering and the losers jeering,
In the ancient Greek Olympics.

In the ancient Greek Olympics,
I can feel the excitement of the crowd
As the winners get announced,
And I can feel the ground as I push myself up,
In the ancient Greek Olympics.

Andrew Cockling (9)
St Mary's RC Primary School, Newcastle upon Tyne

The Ancient Greek Olympics

I'm ready to see
To see the boxing
To see the strong men attacking each other
To see who is to win, who is to lose
I'm ready to see

I'm ready to smell
To smell the Greek ox
To smell the ox's blood
I'm ready to smell

I'm ready to taste
To taste the meat of the ox
To taste the blood of the ox
I'm ready to taste

I'm read to feel
To feel the fire of the Olympics
To feel the king of the gods, Zeus
I'm ready to feel

I'm ready to hear
To hear the boxing audience shouting
To hear the prayers to Zeus
I'm ready to hear.

Kai Zheng (9)
St Mary's RC Primary School, Newcastle upon Tyne

The Snail

Sammy snail
Slithers slowly in the mud
Down below
Eating worms for his tea
That's how he likes to be.

Stephanie Archer (7)
St Mary's RC Primary School, Newcastle upon Tyne

Spring, Oh Spring

Spring, oh spring!
The bells all ring,
Red robins sing,
While oak trees swing.

Smell Miss Tulip
And Miss Rose.
Watch and see . . .
How Miss Sunflower grows.

Streams and lakes
Flow to and fro.
In the sky . . .
There's a rainbow!

The sun is boiling,
Yellow, orange and red.
Shine on them,
The flower bed.

Spring, oh spring!
How you dearly sing,
How you kindly give us
Our daily things . . .

Ikenna Azodo (10)
St Mary's RC Primary School, Newcastle upon Tyne

A Star's Born

Nine years ago when I was born
There was a twinkle in Dad's eye.
I grew and grew and before long
I was more than four foot high.
I sing and dance, I love to perform
Everyone said a star was born.

Tia Radix-Callixte (9)
St Mary's RC Primary School, Newcastle upon Tyne

The Ancient Greek Olympics

In Olympia I see
There are men playing javelin
I see people chanting at the stadium
I see an ox getting slaughtered.

In Olympia I hear
I hear the oxen lowing
I hear people's shouting at boxing
I hear people celebrating.

In Olympia I taste
I taste the meat of oxen
I taste victory everywhere
I taste lots of animals.

In Olympia I feel
I feel nerves for the battle
I feel brilliant for winning
I feel sad.

In Olympia I smell
I smell sweat of boxing
I smell oxen getting burnt
I smell the fire.

Harry Brown (9)
St Mary's RC Primary School, Newcastle upon Tyne

A Pizza

The spicy squishy smell of the pizza
With bread is made from wheat
Cooked in the hot oven
So crusty and crispy
Round as a Frisbee
Specially made for someone to gobble up.

Dylan Armstrong (7)
St Mary's RC Primary School, Newcastle upon Tyne

The Ancient Greek Olympics

The great games of Olympia,
I can feel the ground shaking fiercely as the games go on,
A soft breeze brushing against my face,
Nerves in the air as it gets tense,
The great games of Olympia.

The great games of Olympia,
I can hear the heartbeat of the pensive fans,
The hooves of the horses rattling in the chariot racing,
The crackling fire from the oxen cooks,
The great games of Olympia.

The great games of Olympia,
I can see the bloody wounds of the athletes competing,
Sharp javelins being thrown across the fresh, green grass,
Golden statues of Greek gods,
The great games of Olympia.

The great games of Olympia,
I can taste the sweaty air from the willing competitors,
The burnt flesh of the oxen meat,
The anticipation of the competitors,
The great games of Olympia.

Francesca Booth (9)
St Mary's RC Primary School, Newcastle upon Tyne

My VW Camper Van

Its badge twinkled like the stars on a hot summer's night,
Its paintwork burned in the sunlight like a ball of fire,
The number plate glistened in the beaming light,
The vibrant red carpets and upholstery gave the cab a real plush feel,
The engine rattled like a roller coaster flying down the hill,
Its lights shone as he drove me home!

Carolyn McQueen (10)
St Mary's RC Primary School, Newcastle upon Tyne

The Ancient Greek Olympics

In great Olympia I saw
A fellow competitor, oh how his muscles were so big
I saw all the baby oxen being rounded up to be slaughtered
I saw the statue of almighty Zeus
In great Olympia I saw.

In great Olympia I heard
The chanting and taunts of everyone around me
I heard the complaints of losing and tiredness
I heard the victorious sound of glory
In great Olympia I heard.

In great Olympia I smelt
The terrible smell of burnt, dead oxen
I smelt the awful smell of sweaty athletes
I smelt the glorious smell of victory
In great Olympia I smelt.

In great Olympia I tasted
The burnt oxen meat
I tasted the sweat on my brow
I tasted the sweet taste of glory and bitter defeat
In great Olympia I tasted.

Olivia McCready (10)
St Mary's RC Primary School, Newcastle upon Tyne

Bee World

Wings a-swinging
Backs a-stinging
Fat bees around the planet
I have a pet bee called Janet
They live in a hive
Where they do a bee jive
And they learn to drive.

Rhiannon Parry (7)
St Mary's RC Primary School, Newcastle upon Tyne

The Missing Children

T oday a child may disappear
H ow many is that a year?
E ven with the police alert, that child may still get hurt

M any parents get worried for years
I f their children are not safely returned
S ee them weep on TV
S ee that they want to see their child again safely
I f an adult went away, they would be back in a day
N ever has a child been back so soon
G o and look, it's not true, because lost children's parents are not
    over the moon

C ome and gather around the TV
H ow can parents not be angry?
I f a children's group runs away
L ove is sent right away
D on't stop just because you can't find
R emember the child, keep them in mind
E very day a child is found, turn on the TV
N ever has a policeman said,
    'I give up,' he goes and encourages the family!

Megan Frazer (10)
St Mary's RC Primary School, Newcastle upon Tyne

A Flower

Flowers, flowers
Come out to play
I like it when
I can smell you in the spring
Shiny blossom coming out
The bees are buzzing
Oh, beware of the bees.

Lucy Wood (7)
St Mary's RC Primary School, Newcastle upon Tyne

The Ancient Greek Olympics

All hail almighty Zeus
I can see a javelin surging through the sky
I can see a competitor swearing an oath
To the statue of Zeus.

All hail almighty Zeus
I can hear the grunting of the oxen
I can hear the screaming of the crowd
And the pounding of thousands of feet.

All hail almighty Zeus
I can smell the burning of the oxen bones and fat
I can smell the sweet smell of the sticky sweat
Of other competitors.

All hail almighty Zeus
I can feel the sharp grains of sand
As they get kicked up by the wrestlers
I can feel the ground shaking
As the chariots rumble through the hippodrome
All hail almighty Zeus.

Sergio Olivares (9)
St Mary's RC Primary School, Newcastle upon Tyne

Suspense

The glimmering ball of sunlight skimmed gracefully across the net
As the dazzling moonlight glittered nearby at the dawn of midnight.
The girl ran in the possibility of a match loss,
Desperate to reach the falling tennis ball.
Her sweat dripped forcefully, like a broken tap,
As her joyful opponent smelt a win in her favour.
Just as the shining moonlight turned to the neutraliser,
The suspense was ominous for both of the competitors.
Would she win or lose?

Stephanie Booth (10)
St Mary's RC Primary School, Newcastle upon Tyne

This Is Me

Football player
PS3 player
Computer player
Dog lover
Blue eyes
Jack's brother
Sweet lover
Newcastle supporter
Dog player
Dog stroker
Jamie: friend
Charlie: friend
Cameron: friend
Tennis player
Tennis lover
Football lover
And that adds up to Sam!

Sam Hodgson (8)
St Mary's RC Primary School, Newcastle upon Tyne

A Day At The Farm

One lonely lamb looking for a mate,
Two newborn ducklings swimming in a lake,
Three friendly pigs messing in the mud,
Four naughty donkeys trying to be good,
Five lazy cows lying in the sun,
Six yellow chicks having lots of fun,
Seven cute kittens chasing a tiny mouse,
Eight crazy goats sprinting round the hen house,
Nine sleepy horses lying in the barn,
Ten tired people cleaning up the farm!

Molly Cochrane (11)
St Mary's RC Primary School, Newcastle upon Tyne

The Ancient Greek Olympics

I'm ready,
I can feel the ground shaking
When all the athletes come to end the race
I'm ready,

I can do this,
I can taste
When they are wrestling
In the sweaty air
I can do this,

The great games of the Greek Olympics,
I can smell the fresh blood from the
Games that they are competing
Against other athletes.
The great games of the Greek Olympics.

Katie Corrigan (10)
St Mary's RC Primary School, Newcastle upon Tyne

Crackers And Cheese!

When I know it's time for bed,
A delicious thought comes to my head.
Crackers and cheese it must be,
Nothing else will do for me.

They are lovely,
They are sweet.
Mixed with butter, they taste a treat!

The crunch of the cracker,
The cream of the cheese.
Makes me go all weak at the knees.

They leave lots of crumbs around the house,
That makes me happy because I'm a *mouse!*

Sarah Envy (10)
St Mary's RC Primary School, Newcastle upon Tyne

Christmas With Santa!

I went to the North Pole to meet Santa Claus
I met all the reindeer and shook all their paws.

We went outside carrying Santa's big fat belly
Throwing snowballs in our big chunky wellies.

We went in Santa's workshop and wrapped up a present
It was so very nice and so very pleasant.

We went into the kitchen and made Christmas cakes
We decorated them with little elves, then caught snowflakes.

We made snow angels and I warmed up me
Then Santa came through, with a nice cup of tea.

Then I went back home and told Mum and Dad
What a great day, I'd had.

Michael James Laidlaw (8)
St Mary's RC Primary School, Newcastle upon Tyne

The Land And The Sea!

I see that the clouds race each other
To the hungry mountain mother.

I see that the aqua-coloured sea
Takes away the land, I smile with glee!

I see that the small town below
Looks like an ant to me; I come to say, 'Hello.'

I see that the mountains above
Eat up the clouds, which they love!

I see that the statue drifts along
Like a swimmer, singing a song.

I see that the sun goes down
It glows red, like the nose of a clown!

Gabriel Mason (11)
St Mary's RC Primary School, Newcastle upon Tyne

Icicles

I hang down from your gutters,
It is me who brings fascination to others.

Until those beams of sun come out,
I'm scared now, I try to shout.

Shout, I cannot, but you will see,
Nobody will ever be like me.

I'll see you again some other day,
So now it's my time to drip away.

I'll see you again somewhere cold,
But it won't be me because I'm too old.

There will be some more, long and tall,
But just like me they're sure to fall.

Katie Protheroe (10)
St Mary's RC Primary School, Newcastle upon Tyne

Adds Up To Me

Cheese eater
Wii player
Plays computer
Arm pumper
Good jumper
Pizza eater
Wrestling player
Good sitter
TV watcher
Likes ice cream
Lives in Dunston
Football player
And that all adds up to me!

Timothy Leonard (7)
St Mary's RC Primary School, Newcastle upon Tyne

At The Beach

The dark sea wobbled over smooth sand
Waving at me with a big blue hand.

Lots of fluffy clouds floated across the sky
Like a family of sheep, flying really high.

A stony statue figure stood in the sea
It was a tower of terror looking straight at me.

Harsh whistling wind was cold against my face
So I ran back home with an untied lace.

Rachael Joanne Laidlaw (10)
St Mary's RC Primary School, Newcastle upon Tyne

The Lonely Children

Missing children, lonely and lost
Mums and dads gone to the past
All alone, by themselves
They saw a ghost
It crept into my room as I played a game
My brother was missing
I saw him kissing so gently
The door slowly crept open . . .

Bethany Taylor (10)
St Mary's RC Primary School, Newcastle upon Tyne

Pixie - Cinquain

Pixie
My guinea pig
She lives in a nice hutch
I love my guinea pig so much
Pixie.

Beth Robson (9)
St Mary's RC Primary School, Newcastle upon Tyne

Flower, Flower

Sweet-smelling
Dancing in the breeze
Swishing very slowly in the garden weeds
When one popped up
Looked everywhere
Then went down again
Someone poured water on the little flower again
Very happy to see.

Emilia Recchia (7)
St Mary's RC Primary School, Newcastle upon Tyne

Butterfly

Butterfly lives in a flower
As I reach out for the flower
It peeps out and wonders
Who I am
Going wild in the air
Wings are curled
Every colour in the world
Whoosh goes the butterfly.

Eleanor Mae Vaughan (8)
St Mary's RC Primary School, Newcastle upon Tyne

Rainbow

A rainbow is a big curve
With lots of bright silver, bronze, brown
It curves all around the world
With lots of colours and decorations
When it rains and the sun shines out very bright
You can see the bright lovely rainbow.

Finn Clark (7)
St Mary's RC Primary School, Newcastle upon Tyne

Rainbows

Rainbows are colourful, shining in the sky,
Rainy or sunny, no matter what time
Rainbows will come out beautiful.
You don't see rainbows as often as can be,
No matter what colour it'll be
As sweet as me.
If you go to the end of the rainbow,
I'm sure you will find a pot of gold.

Ellen Williamson (8)
St Mary's RC Primary School, Newcastle upon Tyne

My Flower

I have a sweet-smelling smell
And when spring comes
Lots more flowers grow
And a lot of flowers go dotty
And have bumpy petals
Beware
I have bees
That could sting you.

Mia Clark (7)
St Mary's RC Primary School, Newcastle upon Tyne

Cheeky Monkey

I think monkeys are rather nice
Their tails are long and their faces are small
They run about on the ground all night
And swing through the trees, so tall
But the cheekiest monkeys in those trees
Just have to be the chimpanzees.

Imogen Gray (9)
St Mary's RC Primary School, Newcastle upon Tyne

Monkeys · Haiku

Monkeys in the trees
Brown, big, scary, Japanese
Smelly, dumb, hairy.

Jack Spreadbury (9)
St Mary's RC Primary School, Newcastle upon Tyne

Cake · Haiku

I like my big cake
Flavoured icing smothered on
Eat me up, yum, yum!

Ellen Mary Frisken (8)
St Mary's RC Primary School, Newcastle upon Tyne

Chocolate Chips · Haiku

Melting chocolate chips
Sticky, gooey, yumminess
Yum, yum, in my tum!

Thomas Campion (9)
St Mary's RC Primary School, Newcastle upon Tyne

Flower

Little flower growing so high
Bulbs below in the snow
They look so nice from the window.

Rachael Joyce (8)
St Mary's RC Primary School, Newcastle upon Tyne

Puzzles · Haiku

Puzzles are great fun
They can be for anyone
Puzzles are good games.

Ogochukwu Azodo (9)
St Mary's RC Primary School, Newcastle upon Tyne

The Winter Sunset Window

Draw back the curtains.
Maybe outside there's
A frozen sun or a
Velvet white sky,
Or a robin with
Icicles from his chin.
Draw back the curtains.
Maybe there will be
Black ice stalking
Its prey or maybe
Children screaming
And playing, as the
Frozen fog
Crawls towards
Them.
Draw back the curtains
If you please
Keep the window closed
Or you will freeze.

Georgia Wright (9)
St Paul's RC Primary School, Billingham

Imagine

Imagine a pig
Dressed as the stig

Imagine a dog
Smooching a frog

Imagine a bat
Wearing a hat

Imagine a fox
Sat in a box

Imagine a snake
Baking a cake

Imagine a flamingo
Playing bingo

Imagine me as a bee.

Francesca Holden (8)
St Paul's RC Primary School, Billingham

Imagine

Imagine a dog
eating a log,
Imagine a wasp
Eating candyfloss,
Imagine a skunk
Looking like a hunk,
Imagine a snake
As long as a lake,
Imagine a rabbit
Having a bad habit,
Imagine a bee drinking tea,

And a butterfly eating my pie.

Thomas James Bennett (9)
St Paul's RC Primary School, Billingham

123

Imagine

Imagine a skunk
Dressed as a punk

Imagine a parrot
Eating a carrot

Imagine a bird
Settling a herd

Imagine a bear
Without any hair

Imagine a squid
Having a hundred quid

Imagine a mole
Scoring a goal

Imagine me as a bee.

Jack Lee (9)
St Paul's RC Primary School, Billingham

The Moon

Hovering in the air like
A hawk stalking its prey.
Its night vision eyes stare at the world,
Before it is replaced by a
Golden sparrow.

George Evans (9)
St Paul's RC Primary School, Billingham

Imagine

Imagine a hen
As big as a pen,
Imagine a fish
As big as a dish,
Imagine a squid
Using a quid,
Imagine a fox
Living in a box,
Imagine a frog
Barking like a dog,
Imagine a horse
As long as a golf course,

And imagine a fly
Dressed like a spy.

Lauren Robinson (9)
St Paul's RC Primary School, Billingham

The Final View

Draw back the curtains, maybe there's a dark sun
Or a race of dominating rats,
Or a timid child shivering,

Draw back the curtains, maybe rusty grey ashes
Raining from the white blank sky,
Birds screaming for the final time,
Spitting fire erupting from the hollow ground,

Draw back the curtains if you dare
And see to your now poor world,

Draw back the curtains even if you're scared
You can't escape
From the end.

Jack Greenan (9)
St Paul's RC Primary School, Billingham

Imagine

Imagine a giraffe
Sat in a bath,
Imagine a pig
Dressed as a stig,
Imagine a bug
Giving a hug,
Imagine a snake,
Drinking a lake,
Imagine a fish
Granting a wish,
Imagine a fox
Eating a box,
And a fly saying goodbye!

Brooke Hewson (9)
St Paul's RC Primary School, Billingham

The Stormy Sea Window

Draw back the curtains.
Maybe outside there's
A bellowing wave, or a roller coaster sea,
Or echoing thunder.
Draw back the curtains.
Maybe there's a moon searchlight protecting
The children of the sea
Or a breaking cliff hanging off the edge of
The stormy sea.
Draw back the curtains.
If you dare, the bombing birds will always care.
Draw back the curtains,
Even if the storm goes on into the mist.

Laura Bowman (8)
St Paul's RC Primary School, Billingham

Dragon

Fire breather
Colossal lizard
High flyer
Vicious reptile
Meat lover.

Alistair Twomey (8)
St Paul's RC Primary School, Billingham

The Mummy's Broken Leg

There was an old mummy who
Lived in a shoe,
He broke his leg and didn't know
What to do,
So he went to the doctor's and
The doctor said,
'We'll bandage it up and send
You to bed,'
When the mummy got home he said,
'Have you got a broken leg too?
We can always fix it with some glue.

Riannah Kettlewell (8)
Saltburn Primary School, Saltburn By The Sea

Haikus

Egypt: very hot
Egypt is very sandy
The prince of Egypt

Gold and silver kings
Pharaohs were ruling people
Scarab beetles, old.

Daniella Duncan (8)
Saltburn Primary School, Saltburn By The Sea

The Ancient Egyptian Life

Scarab beetles flying now,
Pyramids and temples being built,
Rameses has become pharaoh,
Seth has fallen,
Oh my goodness,
The slaves are collecting water and are foraging,
Rameses orders lots of food,
He says he is starving,
So he says,
It is night now,
Time for us to go to bed.

Nathaniel Garland (9)
Saltburn Primary School, Saltburn By The Sea

The Egyptian Life

Pharaohs and Gods
Are lazy all day.
'You're the one who
serves me today.'
Rameses runs through
The town with his chariot.
And Moses follows behind.
Mummies are wrapped in bandages.
Is there a mummy around today?
Days have passed, the pharaoh is dead.
Seti has died at last.

Eden Walker (8)
Saltburn Primary School, Saltburn By The Sea

The Worried Mummy

There was an old mummy who lived in a coffin
Just one day when he was scoffin'
A big apple pie,
A spider came down and scared him away
One day he saw the river Nile
So he called the fire brigade on speed dial
The fire brigade came in a hurry
And the mummy said, 'I want a dummy.'
When the River Nile rose up to the mummy's thigh
Oh my goodness, you should have seen him cry!

Lauren Wallis (9)
Saltburn Primary School, Saltburn By The Sea

Naughty Egyptians

E gyptians work day and night.
G etting ready to give Pharaoh a fright!
Y ou will never know what they will do.
P erhaps they will put glue on pharaoh's shoes
T o stick him to the ground so he does not go whipping people
    around.
I would let him go but I would be too slow
A nd I bet Pharaoh doesn't want this to happen again.
N ow it's time to go.
S see you soon!

Mia Schwec (8)
Saltburn Primary School, Saltburn By The Sea

Life Of A Pharaoh

Aten relaxed in his temple,
Holding banquets all night long,
Eating lots and lots,
While wearing lots of jewellery,
When his time is over,
Time to get bandaged up,
With a scarab amulet,
The throne has been passed,
Onto a new pharaoh.

Matthew Hollingworth (8)
Saltburn Primary School, Saltburn By The Sea

Scarab Beetles

Scarab beetles dance all day long
They go across the river Nile
And they go *plong! Plong! Plong!*
Then they sing a jolly song
As they go along
Li li di di li li la la the scarab beetles go to bed
But before they do they do a little dance
Hop hop bong bong jiggle jiggle jam jam
Then they go to bed.

Sophie Iliaifar (9)
Saltburn Primary School, Saltburn By The Sea

Warm Days

W arm, scorching days
A man swims whilst sweating
R ain, it rains not a lot
M ummies wrapped up in a coffin.

Ellie Young (8)
Saltburn Primary School, Saltburn By The Sea

Cleopatra

C leopatra rules Egypt
L azy pharaoh bosses slaves about
E xpensive perfume wafts about
O ld slaves work
P haraohs are bossy
A ncient mummies
T ired slaves
R elieved mummy skulls
A live people serving.

William Trundley (9)
Saltburn Primary School, Saltburn By The Sea

Egyptians Work Day And Night

E gyptians worked day and night.
G etting bricks from out of sight.
Y ears went passed as they worked so hard,
P raying in the fountain yards,
T ime went by so slowly,
I n the yard of the slaves people went so poorly
A nd in the desert
N o one knew,
S lowly snakes rattled their tails two by two.

Alice McMullan (9)
Saltburn Primary School, Saltburn By The Sea

The Sand Storm

S and blows away
A cross the desert
N ile flows everywhere
D onkeys carry hay on their backs.

David Spence (9)
Saltburn Primary School, Saltburn By The Sea

Egyptian Poem

E gyptians work day and night.
G iants, giants, big and bad!
Y ou can see pyramids everywhere.
P yramids are all around.
T reasure can be found underground.
I nside the pyramid there are hieroglyphics.
A ll around there is yellow sand.
N o more mummies were ever seen!

Jasmine Turner-Grierson (9)
Saltburn Primary School, Saltburn By The Sea

Egypt

P haraoh rules Egypt.
Y oung children don't do work as much.
R iver Nile is long.
A nts live in Egypt.
M ums look after their children more.
I n pyramids there are mummies.
D ead bodies.
S and is blown by the wind.

Kyia Taylor-Pawass (9)
Saltburn Primary School, Saltburn By The Sea

The Crazy Pharaoh

The mighty pharaoh, as cool as can be
Goes to the palace and has bread for his tea
He can't eat anything he's got toothache
He goes to the bakery, he has a cake
He hates the cake,
And destroys the bakery!

Oscar Taylor (8)
Saltburn Primary School, Saltburn By The Sea

Pyramids

P yramids glowing in the hot sun
Y our pyramids are hot and sandy
R ain never falls in Egypt
A round Egypt the sun's hot
M ummies get wrapped up
 I n Egypt the sand is very hot
D esert is hot
S and is hot.

Hannah Pollard (8)
Saltburn Primary School, Saltburn By The Sea

Egypt

P haroahs rule the land
Y ellow sand everywhere
R umours give the people a big fright
A man called Moses was the prince of Egypt
M ummies were walking clumsily
 I nside the pyramids lays a stupid mummy, they might
D o something now.

Jay Hampton (8)
Saltburn Primary School, Saltburn By The Sea

The Egyptians

B eetles beetles
E verywhere
E gyptians wear
T heir scarab
L ucky charms
E veryone worships the
S un Gods.

Aiden Paterson (9)
Saltburn Primary School, Saltburn By The Sea

The Scarab Beetle God

Scarab beetle, scarab beetle God
A big, big scarab beetle
The scarab beetle God
Push the sun
Ow, ow, ow, my eyes hurt in the sunlight
What a sight. That's the biggest
Scarab beetle I've seen in my life.

Zoe Johnson (8)
Saltburn Primary School, Saltburn By The Sea

The Mummy

M orning and night, the mummy might give you a fright
U nder the ground they lay, all night and day
M ighty they look, but they aren't as scary as a pirate with a hook
'M ummy, we're over there, behind you, oh no!' we shout and run out
of the pyramid
Y es! We get away, phew that was close, oh no, here he is again.
Yikes! Here he is again.

Lewis Jefferson (8)
Saltburn Primary School, Saltburn By The Sea

Pyramid

P yramid rapidly crumbles in the sun
Y ank the gold from the people's tombs
R ameses sent the Hebrews away
A miracle happened from God
M oses turned the Nile to blood
I sis is the God of the sun
D ead Hebrews lay on the floor.

Ocean Clarke (8)
Saltburn Primary School, Saltburn By The Sea

What Are Camels?

C amels are like a car.
A ctive in their own special way.
M ischievous.
E legant.
L azy.
S andy days, hot and sticky, camels walk through it all.

Olivia Richmond (8)
Saltburn Primary School, Saltburn By The Sea

A Hard Day's Work

E gyptians, Hebrews, work day and night
G ods look over the country trying to keep the people safe
Y ou're not liking your job
P yramids glistening in the golden sun
T ombs getting built in the boiling sun.

Isabel Myers (9)
Saltburn Primary School, Saltburn By The Sea

The Pharaoh

He's the most important person in Egypt
He wears a fake beard and a wig
No one argues with him because
He's pharaoh of Egypt, now all
Bow down to the king.

Betsy Murphy (8)
Saltburn Primary School, Saltburn By The Sea

Mummy Gets Scared

M orning and night mummy gives you a fright
U nder the coffin he goes
M um is frightened
M ummy gets scared, he goes away
Y our whole world watches.

Paul Froom (8)
Saltburn Primary School, Saltburn By The Sea

Egypt's Heat

Egypt was so bright
A man walked to the light
There his flesh burnt, Ra took his soul
All that lay was blood, guts and all.

Thomas Fish (8)
Saltburn Primary School, Saltburn By The Sea

Crocodiles

N o one goes to the Nile where crocodiles smile
I ntelligent, hungry, angry are they
L eaping in the air, there's a smile in the Nile
E xotic fruit grows in May.

Carl Stonehouse (8)
Saltburn Primary School, Saltburn By The Sea

Alien Vegmecet Force

Down on planet Vegmecet
Lived an alien called Noodle
His best friend was Blobvige
And the director was called Coodle.

On planet Vegmecet they planted carrots,
They had been doing this non-stop.
Oh we forgot to tell you about the aliens parrots.
They just think they can plop about
But Noodle thinks they are tops.

Now I'll tell you about the broccoli,
They're also known as trees.
Hey let's play some Monopoly,
Now I'm going to describe the peas.

Peas, glorious peas,
Just how do they make them?
Not like your trees,
In our solar system.

Out they flew
To the planet Noglo
Where their faces
Turned blue.

Now they were as
Happy as can be.
Their heart was full of love.

Holly Buck & Laura Grady (10)
Tarleton CE Primary School, Tarleton

Aliens On Mars

I'm wearing my shiny spacesuit
And sitting in my chair
I'm waiting for my rocket to blast me
Off into the air!

I'm zooming past the planets, whizzing
Past the stars
Heading to my destination,
The red planet, Mars.

Pulling on the brakes, preparing now to land,
There are lots of funny aliens
Dancing on the sand.

Turn off the engine, open the door
Out I get ready to explore!
Searching around, with a heart full of fear,
The aliens look scary now I'm near!

I find out in seconds that the
Aliens aren't nice,
If you dare to touch their skins you will
Freeze like ice!

The aliens are so bad they leave me
On a rock,
And leave me a clock there
To *tick-tock-tick-tock!*

What to do? Got to get out,
But no, it is no use
I will have to shout!

'Help! Help! Help!' I'll never get out,
Maybe I could trick them
Into letting me out!

I have a plan! Hooray for me
Will it work? We'll have to see.

I give them a candy
Then they drop out dead
What good thinking
From my clever head!

Back in the rocket, time to blast off,
Now, for Jupiter
Let's hop off.

Woo! Look at this
It's something you can't miss
I can't believe my eyes,
No I'm not telling lies!

The spaceship is dead
We can't get back
Let's just hope we're not under attack!

There is as spaceman here,
He's come to save us
Let's go back to Earth after a ride on his
Space bus!

Gabriel Gouveia & Glenn Sherwin (10)
Tarleton CE Primary School, Tarleton

Inside Zog

I was sat in my rocket
Wondering where to go
I thought very carefully
Then I said, 'I'll go to Pluto'
So off I went
Above the tallest tree
And then I relaxed
With a nice iced tea.

All the way to Pluto
I flew in my rocket
But then I remembered
I forgot my best locket
Then I looked at my map
I was nearly there
And when I got out of the ship
Something pulled my hair.

When I looked around I saw an alien
Looking me in the eye
And then I heard his booming voice
Say, 'You, you're going to die!'

He was as green as a marsh
It was very, very ick
And when he swallowed me
I was nearly sick!

The alien boomed, 'My name is Zog'
And me being inside him it was even louder
I needed to get out quick
And that made him even prouder
I couldn't stand it any longer
So I wiggled and slid
And then I heard Zog say
'It feels like my two tummy's have collided.'

His tummy was extremely wet
And it was a swimming pool
It must have been very uncomfortable
Having a tummy full of drool
Then I remembered my gun
I was aiming to shoot
But it wouldn't work
Like my car boot!

After hours of struggling
I finally got out
And I'm never coming back
Not while he's about
And next time I think
Where shall I go
I am very sure
It won't be Pluto!

Emily Jones & McKenzie Mitchell (10)
Tarleton CE Primary School, Tarleton

Adventure With Frank, Bob And Tank

There was once an alien called Bob
And his friend's name was Frank
What was the other one's name?
Oh yes, his name was Tank.

They were going on a journey
To planets near and far
To celebrate the occasion they said
'Hip, hip, he, he, hoorah!'

First they went to Pluto
the commander said, 'It's so small!'
Their planet was a different shape
Pluto was a round ball.

Next they flew to Neptune.
And froze 1000 miles away.
The ice was as hard as granite,
so they were still there yesterday!

The ice finally melted,
so they sped to Uranus
It was as gross as bottom burps,
so they got back on the space bus.

They were now worked out and tired,
no energy for more travel.
They were going home because,
they were sick of eating space gravel.

They were nearly at their home,
when they saw an unusual thing.
It gave out a loud, *moo,*
and something on its neck went *ding-a-ling.*

They also saw another thing,
to you and me, a penguin.
They were amazed with this creature,
and thought it was extremely genuine!

When they got home, Frank and Tank *stank!*

Abbie Crawford (9) & Amy Rose Goymer (10)
Tarleton CE Primary School, Tarleton

Space Poem

We were standing in a rocket,
When I tripped with my hand in my pocket.
We hit the launch lever,
And on board with us was a beaver.

While losing all gravity,
And speeding away,
We finally made it to space,
So we shouted, 'hip, hip, hooray!'

We were getting quite hungry,
So I said to Sam,
'We've got some food with us
so try to cook us some spam.'

We were soaring through the sky,
Heading for Orb 9,
But I think we went a bit too high,
And missed it by a mile.

Then we saw a giant rock,
As big as a flat block.
We were going to start heading,
But oops, I nearly forgot, it was our annual wedding.

Leo Beard & Kelsey Fairclough (9)
Tarleton CE Primary School, Tarleton

A Space Adventure

We flew up high into the sky
After we said goodbye
Racing towards outer space at our own pace
We thought it was ace.

Blasting through the stars
Welcome to Mars
And saw aliens driving cars
At midnight we passed a crater full of data
We thought that we would go later.

We set off to a planet much bigger than our own
We saw something in the distance
It looked like an alien clone
They started to double
We hopped on board and found a couple
Of hover boards belonging to the time lords.

We said goodbye and set off for Saturn
We weren't quite sure but we were told they spoke Latin
They told us of a planet named Zog
Which was full of fog.

Time to go homeward bound
In another hour we'll be hitting the ground
We've landed safe and sound
We told the people what we found.

Ned Melling & Tom Robinson (9)
Tarleton CE Primary School, Tarleton

Saturn Invades

Tom and Jim were doing garden work,
Until they found a mysterious button.
They pressed the button and were in hyperspace,
Which took them to planet Saturn.

They looked across and found a race,
Which was heading for the west.
Tom then said, 'Let's go and follow
As we support for the best.'

They followed them to a big red castle
And met the King which caused a hassle.
Tom and Jim said, 'Can we join?'
'Yes but do have a coin?'

Jim showed the coin to the King
And then the king went, 'Cha-Ching!'
On the third day the war had began,
And the Saturn people used a frying pan.

Both armies clashed head to head
And the king fled when half of his men were dead.
The evil king headed to Earth
To capture a boy who was having his birth.

Dylan Brookes (9) Alex Casey
Tarleton CE Primary School, Tarleton

Invaded By Humans

Oak, Chestnut and Maple were sitting by the Forbound Lake,
It was a dazzling beauty no one could mistake.
Mercury was a land of trees;
Everything was amazing see,
Even though it might make you sneeze.

Somewhere near the amazing star cave,
A massive rocket went *crash, bang, zoom.*
Oak was thinking of a brand new slave,
But to the trees' surprise,
The human was an evil snake,
And I'm not telling you a lie.

Out came Pine and his furious looking gang.
Pine could not get scarier; he was a scary as can be.
The humans were so scared because Pine had a fang.
Pine backed them into the rocket, they ran so fast.
It was extremely frightening,
However, thankfully now it was in the past.

Oak was so happy; he was jumping about with glee,
Everyone was completely delighted,
The baby said, 'They won't come back to get me!'

Maggie Harrison (9) & Robyn Hipwell (10)
Tarleton CE Primary School, Tarleton

The Capture!

As Jack and Ben left Earth in their rocket,
They just put their hands in their pocket.
They headed west as they landed on Mars.
They held on to shiny metal bars.

As they got out the rocket they looked behind
And their rocket was tied down.
They started to frown.

As they explored the place,
An alien said, 'want a race?'
'Yes,' The astronaut agreed.
Then the alien said, 'If you win you shall be free.'

The astronauts were so fast,
And off they went in a blast.
The astronauts won and the alien said,
'You are free.'
But they were very angry.

As the astronauts headed home,
They looked at Earth, it was in a dome.

Ben Ritson (9) & Jack Marsh (10)
Tarleton CE Primary School, Tarleton

Journey To Mars

Climbing in a rocket flying over the sea,
All of a sudden Ryan banged his knee,
Ryan and the rest of the gang were as thin as a snail,
But when they were halfway there Leon and Lewis ate their first pea.
When they landed on Mars they saw something really strange,
And then an alien walked past
It looked like a she.
All of the stuff looked like bombs
Then there was a speech that was a plot to destroy Earth
Then Ryan said, 'Let's all go to the beach.'
But when they were just about to leave the aliens chased after them
So they left quickly as they paced away
In the control room they fired up the engines.
But the aliens fired up their engines and chased
As they raced around the universe
They were almost at Earth
But an asteroid was going to hit Earth
As they hit the asteroid they blocked it
Then they landed in Yorkshire.

Peter Stockwin, Ryan Stansfield & Lewis Joughin (9)
Tarleton CE Primary School, Tarleton

Blast-Off To Saturn

We set off to space
Passed all the planets on the way
We reached Saturn, our destination
As cold as an icy day.

Luckily I had hand warmers
And was wearing my thermal underwear
So I was as warm as toast
And an alien was there.

Then we heard a voice from behind
It sounded like a witch's cry
We turned around and saw them snarl and fly.
We jumped into our rockets and zoomed to Pluto,
Where we felt safe in the caves below.

We zoomed back up to Pluto,
Stuart looked so tall and Pluto looked so small
We played on Pluto and then zoomed off home!

Stuart Edge & Thomas Usher (9)
Tarleton CE Primary School, Tarleton

Robots V Aliens

25 astronauts set off in the shuttle,
Bound for Uranus, way past Hubble.
They looked out of the window and
Saw a planet that looked as clear as glass,
And remembered they had learnt about
This planet in astronaut class.

50 Martians appeared in a bubble,
The astronauts laughed and that spelt trouble.
The Martians came to earth and looked around,
They flattened all the buildings without making a sound.

The astronauts came back and they were shocked,
They built 100 robots to kill the lot.
The Martians, they were vaporised and the astronauts cheered,
They jumped for joy because they realised the Earth was saved for a
million years.

Rebecca Singleton (10) & Ben McLaughlan (9)
Tarleton CE Primary School, Tarleton

Alien Adventure To Emgor

Deep in the woods a spaceship flew,
It was circling above us as fast as space knew.
We were transported to where we saw a Goblin pressing a switch.
Zoom, past Venus, past Mercury
Until we came to the sun,
Golly gosh, that was fun!
Into a small planet, past the sun,
We landed and we spun, spun, spun and spun.
Shoved into an intergalactic prison
With mega tall doors
With a shake and a bang something happened,
It must have been a meteor . . .
The next thing we were in bed
It must have been a dream, we all classified it
As a dream instead.

Thomas Sinclair (9) & Jack Southern (10)
Tarleton CE Primary School, Tarleton

Adventure To Mars

In space a rocket shot,
Getting near the sun it got a bit too hot.
So they headed to Mars
They found out they had no bars.
So they landed on Mars and saw a hole as big as a crater.
They got our of their rocket and later
They saw an alien dictator.

They went further on and around
A hole as black as coal
So they went down and found aliens
With their faces upside down!
They ran back to their rocket
With their hands in their pockets
And shot back to Earth in a second
But they forgot their flag.

Tom Marsh & Leon Wignall (10)
Tarleton CE Primary School, Tarleton

Thunderstorm

A storm tastes like a sour sweet
A storm feels like a very cold iron
It sounds like a pebble hitting the ground
And feels like metal on my leg
And smells like soggy, wet grass
It looks like light hitting off the ground
It's as scary as a haunted house
It tastes as hard as iron
And sounds like a loud whistle.

Elenor Robe (11)
Tynedale Middle School, Blyth

The Storm

A storm tastes like pickled onions
A storm feels like sandpaper
It sounds like children screaming
And smells like burning rubber
It's as scary as a vampire
It tastes as sour as sherbet
And it sounds as loud as a lion
It feels like ice falling down your back
It looks like shattered glass.

Jayne Douglass (12)
Tynedale Middle School, Blyth

The Storm

A storm tastes like damp rain
A storm feels like wet sand
It sounds like basketballs
And feels like rust
It looks like lightning smashing off the ground
And smells like burnt food
It's scary as a roaring tiger
It tastes as sour as a lemon
And sounds as loud as a car horn.

Shelby Elise Shepherd (11)
Tynedale Middle School, Blyth

The Storm

A storm tastes like ice-cold steel.
A storm feels like sandpaper.
It sounds like an explosion in the sky
And feels like limestone.
It looks like thousands of rays of light hitting the floor in seconds
And smells like burning wood.
It is as scary as an out of control fire in woodland.
It tastes as if you're swallowing glass
And sounds like a missile dropping next to you.

Adam Hartill (11)
Tynedale Middle School, Blyth

The Storm

A storm tastes like gone-off milk.
A storm feels like wet mud.
A storm sounds like the thunder hitting the ground
And it feels like rust.
It looks like thunder
And it smells of burnt food.
It's as scary as a tiger.
It tastes like a sour lollipop
And it sounds like a lion.

Corrie-Anne Hutchinson (11)
Tynedale Middle School, Blyth

The Storm

A storm tastes like burnt food
A storm feels like ice
It sounds like chalk on a squeaky chalkboard
And feels like coal
It looks like high voltage
And smells like cut grass
It's as scary as meeting a zombie
It tastes as hard as rock
And sounds like cymbals dropping.

Kimberley Storey (11)
Tynedale Middle School, Blyth

The Storm

A storm tastes like a hot chocolate
A storm feels like an electric shock
It sounds like a big bang
And feels like ice getting put down your back
It looks like a sparkling light
And smells like fire
It's scary as a monster
It tastes as nice as chips
And sounds as loud as a volcano.

Darren Rutherford (11)
Tynedale Middle School, Blyth

The Storm

A storm tastes like burnt food
A storm feels like rust on an old bike
It sounds like basketballs bouncing
And feels like ice crackling
It looks like a sparkle in the beautiful sky
And smells like smoke coming from an oven
It's as scary as a lion roaring at me
It tastes like burnt cookies
And sounds like horses clapping their hooves.

Karl McLean (11)
Tynedale Middle School, Blyth

The Storm

A storm tastes like roasted hair
A storm feels like the bottom of a shoe
It sounds like a brass band
And feels like a big wave sweeping me away
It looks like a lion going to eat you
And smells like wet socks
It is as scary as the world going to crash into the sun
It tastes like seaweed
And sounds like a big drum.

Ross Bell (11)
Tynedale Middle School, Blyth

The Storm

A storm tastes like metal.
A storm feels like rust.
It sounds like horses galloping
And feels like chunks of sand.
It looks like shattered glass
And smells like fire.
It's as scary as a horror film.
It tastes like damp grass
And sounds like cymbals.

Rachel Mee (12)
Tynedale Middle School, Blyth

Thunderstorm

A storm tastes like hot chocolate
A storm feels like ice
It sounds like a house falling
And feels like sharp pencils
It looks like wire
And smells like fire
It is as scary as a scream
It tastes like chips hitting the floor
And sounds like a car crashing.

Liam Thornton (12)
Tynedale Middle School, Blyth

The Storm

A storm tastes like lollies
A storm feels like soft oranges
It sounds like dripping water
And feels like a hot day
It looks like thunder bouncing off the wall
And smells like apples
It's as scary as the world falling apart
It tastes like sweet lava
And sounds like girls screaming.

Scott Nelson (11)
Tynedale Middle School, Blyth

The Storm

A storm tastes like broccoli
A storm feels like rust on a bike
It sounds like a creaking bike
And smells like damp cork
It's as scary as a roller coaster
It tastes like a mouldy carrot
And sounds like banging.

Isabella Gongas (12)
Tynedale Middle School, Blyth

Young Writers Information

We hope you have enjoyed reading this book - and that you will continue to enjoy it in the coming years.

If you like reading and writing poetry drop us a line, or give us a call, and we'll send you a free information pack.

Alternatively if you would like to order further copies of this book or any of our other titles, then please give us a call or log onto our website at www.youngwriters.co.uk.

A platform for your poetry!

Young Writers Information
Remus House
Coltsfoot Drive
Peterborough
PE2 9JX
(01733) 890066